Tammy

Why Didn't You? Get It Done?

Thanks for all the support.
You know you're the
best cousin in the world.
I love you for inspiring me
and I hope this inspires you to
TAKE ACTION!!!

BARRETT MATTHEWS

Barrett Matthews

Why Didn't You Get It Done?

© 2013 by Barrett Matthews

ISBN: 978-0615739113

Printed in the United States of America

Dedication

I would like to dedicate this book to Ronnett Smith,
a woman who has taught me what real strength,
commitment, and courage it takes to get things done.

Table of Contents

Chapter 1 –
Excuse Me

We all need motivation and encouragement, and I'm here to do just that for you. I am not only an author, I am also a coach. It is in my nature to coach, so it is going to come forth in my writing. I want to start with a quote that came from a fortune cookie; not every fortune cookie has a great saying, but this one was unavoidable.

The piece of paper said, "The secret of getting ahead is getting started."

This is exactly what I did: I got started. Now, I'm continuously moving forward, and I am even getting a little ahead of myself. However, that isn't always a bad thing. If you aren't getting ahead of yourself, you will always be behind everyone else. Before we "get started" on this adventure of making that choice to begin, I want to recognize the five most influential coaches in my life:

1) God – Who set the plan for a wonderful life.

2) My Parents – Who guided me in the right direction, and were always there for me.

3) Friends and Family – Who helped me develop social skills.

4) Peggy and Eric Hightower – Who taught me how to run a tight and accountable ship in business while keeping priorities in order.

5) Trevor Otts – Who taught me about marketing myself (branding myself), and my talents to get the maximum results.

I couldn't have started anything without God, who set the plan for a wonderful life. You see, even if **you** don't yet have a "plan" for your life, God does. Jeremiah 29:11 says that "God plans to prosper us and not harm us, and He has a hope and a future," for each one of us. Even if you have to start your life over from scratch, don't be dismayed. Life is all about building up, tearing down, and rebuilding again. The times when life is "tearing down," while it seems as if everything is gone, you really haven't lost anything. Maybe you have lost your job, your family, or your entire life.

Remember Job in the Bible? God took everything away from him, but after Job passed the test, God gave him so much more. It's the same now: Just pass the test, keep on moving, and you will see a brand new day.

Brooding and sulking over what was lost will only slow you down and lessen your motivation. As they say, "God cannot steer a ship that isn't moving." Even if you don't like where you are, keep moving, and don't stop. God will steer you in the right direction. He is in control at all times, even when you believe you are.

Water that only sits in a stream, that isn't flowing, gets murky and muddy-hardly something you would want to bathe in much less drink, unless it starts to move. Do you feel murky? Do you feel that you have been stagnant for way too long?

Once the water gets moving it is purified and drinkable again. If you stay motionless and don't make decisions, then your mind will always be in a place of muddy and stagnant confusion. Even if the decisions you make aren't the correct ones at first, at least you've got the river flowing again, and then your mind will start clearing up so you can think, move, and act in a positive, more productive manner.

So, now we ask the question, "What is the root of the problem?" or "Why aren't I getting things done?" The answer is fairly simple. It's procrastination. Procrastination is not going to get you anywhere, literally. If you wait until you become perfect before you start doing something, anything, then you will never begin. Many people begin projects and keep on going, revising again and again and again. They are never happy, so they keep on redoing it, worrying that it won't be "good enough."

You know what happens to those people? They miss their chance, because someone else has started doing the same thing, and has completed it. It's already out on the market for sale, and the procrastinators wonder how this could've happened.

I'll tell you how it happened; they changed their idea so many times that it either no longer made sense or even applied. The next person stole the spotlight, and rightfully so.

If you have something to give to the world, but then you make everyone wait, they will look elsewhere.

People need what you have. We all need each other's gifts and talents. If you don't get yourself out there in good timing, the people who needed what you "had" have gotten their needs fulfilled by someone else who has gifts and talents similar to yours.

God didn't give you these talents to merely bury in the ground. If you have something in your heart to do, and you don't do it, God will move on to the next person and ask him or her to do it instead. "God isn't calling the qualified, He qualifies the called."

I believe I have been called and qualified. This is merely because I have done what I said I was going to do. I have made plenty of mistakes along the way, but I have learned from them all. You cannot truly learn without making some mistakes, because with each mistake, your technique and your talent get better and better. If I make a mistake, I don't blame anyone or anything else but myself- and I don't make excuses, either.

Some people have accused me of being too harsh, mean, angry, and that I need to take it easy on people. When I'm told these things it is usually because of one glaring theme: I don't take excuses from people. I abhor excuses. If I make a mistake, I don't blame anyone or anything else but myself, and I don't make excuses, either. I take full responsibility for all of my actions.

I don't make excuses, and I take full responsibility for all of my actions. I'm not saying I don't make mistakes at all, because we all do. However, I don't beat around the bush and blame anything or anyone else. I fully admit my wrong, apologize, and don't blame shift.

Here is an example: I once ran a network marketing business. At first I was successful. However, I didn't run my business properly. Years later the business fell down the toilet, so I had to leave it behind. People have come up to me since then and asked, "What happened?" or "Why did you leave the business?"

The first thing I tell them is, "I didn't manage my business properly."

These people are shocked at my answer. I'm sure they expected me to use the excuse that a lot of people use, which is a boldface lie, and that is, "It didn't work out for me."

Let me tell you something, business doesn't "work" for anyone; **you** actually have to "work it." Don't fall for it when you hear that from people. Or others may say, "I didn't get the support I needed" or "My up-line didn't help me." All they are doing is making excuses, shifting blame and not taking responsibility.

The bottom line is; it is your business. If you didn't work your business and it failed, then look in the mirror and see yourself, and yourself, only. You must take responsibility because if you don't, no one else will. If you let other things or other people get in the way of your success, then you decided somewhere along the line that your success wasn't as important to you as other people or things were.

You are the only one who ultimately controlled everything. You are still in control of your life. No one else is. If you failed, then you have to look at yourself, and don't make excuses.

You have probably heard this before: "You can either make excuses or you can make money, but you can't make both."

You have to decide: Which one are you going to do? If you are going make money, then you have to put that childish stuff aside and stop making excuses for things that don't go your way. You have to say, "That is my mistake, and I alone let it happen."

Those who shift blame are afraid of being looked at as failures or as being weak. Just because you make a mistake doesn't mean that you are a failure. If you blame other people or things for getting in your way, you are essentially saying that you had no control over what happened. Others will only view you as a failure if you do shift blame, and if that is the case then you will never be a leader.

Let's say you are in the middle of something that needs to be finished, an assignment, or a deadline of sorts; if you allow other people to interrupt or continue talking to you about something, then you are allowing them to have power over your life. If you can't get up the courage to be honest with them and tell them that you cannot be interrupted, not only will you be behind in completing your work, but you will also be angry at them and at yourself for not saying anything.

What's worse? Being angry and not getting everything finished in time, or being honest, letting your feelings out, and having everything completed?

I'm a leader and I expect people to live up to their potential. I don't expect everyone to follow me, exactly, but I do expect people to follow my leadership qualities. Those include not procrastinating, not wasting time talking, and gossiping, especially you know you have more important things to do, for example, studying and learning information necessary to pass a test or to move forward, or completing whatever work that needs to get done. If you get started on those projects and chores, and get them finished will feel a great sense of relief, and you will also be able to take a break without worrying about what still needs to get done.

Don't think that I don't have a "life" too, because I most certainly do. However, you don't mix business with pleasure, and you shouldn't have fun or relax until after you are finished with your commitments. You may have to work very hard for a certain period of time before you can relax and take breaks. It may not seem fair, but life isn't about being fair. Putting priorities first is a must. I have a "life" too, and am very busy.

However, I get things done, and I don't let anything or anyone deter my focus. If I do allow someone to deter me, it is because "I allowed it" or "I didn't choose to take responsibility." I won't blame them because I didn't complete my project or throw them under the bus. Blaming someone else makes us both look bad, and it makes me look even worse, because the problem may not have been their fault. Instead of blaming, it is important to stop, think, and then wait awhile before speaking.

It may have looked as if the problem was their fault, but if I had made different choices, no matter what the other person did, it wouldn't have mattered. So many times we think that blaming another person will relieve our own consciences, but that isn't true at all. Not only do we know subconsciously when we were at fault, we also know we could have avoided or prevented a problem by doing something else. However, when we choose not to do that "something else," then we are the only ones to blame.

Do you deserve the blame? If you would take a moment and just allow yourself to feel the guilt and blame of your non-actions, just for that short time, you would be able to see it for what it really is – your fault; then you will be able to think of ways to avoid this in the future.

Here is another example: Someone came into my office for a meeting and we had a dress code in the office. He hadn't been told that we had a dress code and came dressed inappropriately.

He asked me, "You're not going to hold that against me are you?"

I said, "No, I'm not going to hold that against you, because the person you talked to and set up this meeting didn't tell you that we have a dress code, so that isn't your fault."

Then he says, "My friend, who was my transportation, didn't have the time to take me home so I could change my clothes."

I said, "Well, I am going to hold that against you."

He said, "What?"

I then told him, "I'm going to hold that against you; you made an excuse by throwing your friend under the bus, as to why you didn't get the right clothes. If you knew that you could have brought clothes with you to change into, you should've had them with you."

You don't throw someone under the bus to make it easier on yourself. That's what most of us try to do; we make so many excuses. People give so many excuses. That's what I hate – excuses.

One excuse that people use is that they are broke. If you don't have the money, I can't change that- I'm sorry. If you say you are broke but you get a new tattoo, or get your hair done, then look at your priorities, and stop making that excuse. You should have said. "I had the money, but I chose to use it on something else."

Other people say they didn't have the time. "I would've gotten there, but I overslept."

Or, "No one woke me up."

They will blame it on the alarm clock. I find it funny that people say they set their alarm clock 20 minutes ahead so that they won't be late. I don't see how that works, who are you fooling? If you set the alarm clock, and you know it is ahead, you hit the snooze knowing you have that extra time, so does it really matter? If you know you had to be somewhere, then make the preparations to be there.

Another excuse many people use is health. "I was sick and couldn't do it," or "I couldn't do it because I was in pain." I have a friend who is a single mother of two children, and the grandmother of two children. She is also attending college for an additional degree, and works three jobs. You might say that is quite impressive. She also has Type 1 diabetes, a preexisting condition that she has had all her life. It is kind of hard to get insurance with a preexisting condition, so she has no health insurance. She also has cancer.

However, she still gets up every day and goes to work, or her classes, or to do something with her children or grandchildren, and she does it with a smile on her face, even if she is in pain and hurting. She still keeps going and doesn't sit there and say, "I can't because." She doesn't give into the excuse monster like many of us tend to do.

Now, that is the type of person that I have the utmost respect for.

Others may use the excuse that they can't do it because they had to work. They will say that they want to start a business, knowing full-well that they don't want to or can't quit their full time job. I don't expect them to quit their jobs, but then why would they come to me for coaching in order to start a business? A person who does this is merely making an excuse as to why they shouldn't do it, instead of just going ahead and doing it.

One of my biggest pet peeves when it comes to excuses is when people use their children as an excuse. Too often I hear, "I can't do it- I have children." I worked with a woman who would constantly shirk her duties, while using the excuse that her child needed her time. Keeping in mind that her child was a good student and well-behaved, she could have taken her child to work with her. But it was more convenient to place the weight on the child and not do the work. People are quick to throw the kid under the proverbial bus, instead of putting their butt on the line and talking to the kid about what the end result is. Most kids will understand what you are attempting to accomplish and will be willing to do their part if you include them and show them the benefit. Don't blame your kid for not doing what you need to do. Your children are an offspring of you, not vice versa. If anything, they should be blaming you for not doing right by them in those instances.

I don't have children myself, but I have a very soft spot for them: They don't get to choose who their parents or grandparents are. They don't get to choose for themselves if they wanted even to be born or not. So, when they do come into this world, at your choice, with your knowledge, then why do you, as parents, make excuses?

If starting a new business will benefit your children, and you want your children to benefit, have a good life, then why wouldn't you just go ahead and do it? Your children should be your motivation above all else. So, why would you throw your children under the bus? Why use them as an excuse NOT to do that which will make a better life for them?

Instead, focus on your children and make them happy. If you can do that, then you will have a better relationship with them and a better life, because you won't be making excuses any longer.

If you say, "I can't do it because my kid needs me to do "such and such." STOP! Speak to your children and tell them the truth; they will understand. Children aren't stupid. They **will** understand. They won't throw a hissy fit if you decide to do something that will benefit them in the long run. If you keep that in mind, you will be fine. Get over yourself. Your kids already have.

Excuses are used to get out of doing things, to make sure you aren't held responsible for failure. Too often, people want a reward for doing something they didn't do; on the other hand, they don't want to pay the consequences for not doing it. Instead, they want to give a rationale as to why they didn't get it done. Are you going to make an excuse, knowing that no one in their right mind is going to believe you, anyway?

"I didn't get that assignment done because my kid got sick last night." Unless your child was in the E.R. then you should have done that assignment. The bottom line is we love to use other people as excuses. It is like we have a constant crutch, but if we keep leaning on that crutch, we will never walk on our own.

That constant crutch is something that will really damage us. We put our thoughts on minor things, instead of focusing on the big picture. The big picture is ultimately what keeps us going. If you focus on the end result, you won't have time to make excuses, because you will be working on your goal and your dream.

A lot of fraternities use the following quote to motivate members: "Excuses are monuments for nothingness, and they build bridges to nowhere. Those of us who use these tools of incompetence, seldom become anything, but nothing at all."

Whatever you focus on is going to grow. So, if you focus on excuses, then excuses are what you will get from life in return.

Quotes on Excuses

"The only thing standing between you and your goal is the bullshit story that you keep telling yourself as to why you can't achieve it." (Jordan Belfort)

"It is better to offer no excuse than a bad one." (George Washington)

"At the end of the day, let there be no excuses, no explanations, and no regrets." (Steve Mariboli)

"Never make excuses. Your friends don't need them, and your foes won't believe them."(John Wooden)

"He that is good for making excuses is seldom good for anything else." (Benjamin Franklin)

"I attribute my success to this: I never gave or took any excuse." (Florence Nightingale)

"The heart has its reasons, but the mind makes excuses." (Amit Abraham)

"There is a lie in between a promise and many excuses." (Toba Beta)

"A man can fail many times, but he isn't a failure until he begins to blame somebody else." (John Burroughs)

"The best day of your life is the one on which you decide your life is your own. No apologies or excuses. No one to lean on, rely on, or blame. The gift is yours – it is an amazing journey – and you alone are responsible for the quality of it. This is the day your life really begins." (Bob Moawad)

"Never ruin an apology with an excuse." (Kimberly Johnson)

"Excuses are tools of the incompetent, and those who specialize in them seldom go far." (C.S. Lewis)

"Nothing is impossible; there are ways that lead to everything, and if we had sufficient will we should always have sufficient means. It is often merely for an excuse that we say things are impossible." (Francois De La Rochefoucauld)

"You can give in to the failure messages and be a bitter deadbeat of excuses. Or you can choose to be happy and positive and excited about life." (A.L. Williams)

"Don't make excuses. Make something incredible happen in your life right now." (Greg Hickman)

A Cautionary Tale – "N"

Norma, just started a job, and she started out training with her new manager. They had to spend a lot of time together, and her manager was very friendly. She wanted to make sure Norma was comfortable with her job.

After a time, Norma became comfortable with her job and started to give excuses for things: unfinished assignments, coming into work late all of the time, and missing meetings.

She gave an excuse every time no matter what the problem was. She gave excuses about her husband's behavior- that he was cheating on her; how they had arguments and he was sabotaging her day.

She thought she was really going to get a promotion when the time came. She thought she and her manager were very close, liked each other, worked well together.

What Norma didn't know was that her manager only remembered her excuses. She remembered Norma's children got in trouble in school and how Norma's car wouldn't start in the winter and that Norma's washing machine broke so she didn't have clean clothes to wear to work one day.

She remembered Norma's excuses, that Norma hadn't learned how to change things to be more productive.

If you want to be productive, successful, and respected, then stop giving excuses.

You can make excuses or you can make money, but you can't make both.

Don't be a Norma.

Chapter 2 –
Better Never Than Late

Have you ever spent your time waiting on someone who never came, or who came so late that you missed everything? I will say that I've spent too much time waiting for others. I cannot stand lateness. Being late is one of the most inexcusable things in the world. Especially when you don't call whoever is waiting for you so they know you are running behind.

Now, some people have legitimate reasons for running behind. Other people give the following reasons for being late:

- To be fashionable
- It's O.K.
- It's cool
- They don't care
- Want attention, even if it is negative

Some people think that being "fashionably late" is the style nowadays. Nothing could be further from the truth. Lateness isn't something you "buy" at the store and "put on." If you could buy lateness, it would be priceless because you can never get that time back, ever again.

In this economic downturn we are currently contending with, if you want to keep your job, you simply can't be late. If you want to get on someone's good side, you should go one step beyond being on time and show up early.

It isn't "o.k." or "cool" to be late. Go to bed an hour earlier and don't watch television late at night so you can get up and get going. Be disciplined. If you show someone that you don't care enough about them to be early, or at least on time, they will feel it, even if only subconsciously. Respect is something you have to earn, and if you are an entrepreneur, you can earn respect easily by being responsible, punctual, and caring.

Everyone conducting business needs to be "noticed," and if you give yourself a good, respectable name, you will be noticed, and then some. If you want attention, you aren't going to get it from me, unless you are on time.

If you are chronically late, and you also have trouble getting things done in your life, then it is obvious as to why. You've heard the expression, "The early bird catches the worm," well, there you go. If you're chronically late you're never going to get the "goods" are you.

There is also a Bible verse (Proverbs 6:10, The Message) that says, "A nap here, a nap there, a day off here, a day off there, sit back take it easy – do you know what comes next? Just this: You can look forward to a dirt poor life, poverty your permanent house guest."

It is also selfish, disrespectful, and rude to be late. Other than death or a major accident, there is no reason to be late. One thing people know about me is that if I'm late, then something must have happened. I hate being late. I'd rather be an hour early than a minute late. I hate waiting for people. If I hate waiting for someone, then how can I be late, myself? I want to do unto others as I would have them do unto me. So, I make sure that I'm on time. I don't want someone else to say, "Well, you are always late." If I hate waiting, then how can I be late, myself?

Being late makes you look irresponsible and completely unprofessional. How can you be a leader, or a business owner, or an entrepreneur if you are always late? You cannot. So, if lateness is your "style," and you have no intention of changing your style, then give up your dreams of being a leader or a business owner. If you know, without a doubt, that you can work on your lateness to the point of eliminating the problem altogether, so you are always on time no matter what, then keep moving forward.

If you have problematic people in your life, and if they are needy, demanding and so forth, you wouldn't leave work in the middle of the day to deal with their issues, would you? Chances are they wouldn't even ask you to deal with their problems in the middle of your work day. So, if you are trying to start your own business, and your family behaves as if you are always "around" and open to dealing with their issues, yet you know you are unavailable and have a lot to do- just as if you were working at a "normal" job, then you must put your foot down.

Talk to them. Let them know that starting a business takes more work than a regular job, and they need to leave you alone.

Another consideration is to ask them for help with things that need to get done. As a leader, you need to learn how to delegate tasks, anyway. Tell them they need to be responsible for themselves, because in order for you to help them, you must first help yourself and put your business at the top of your priority list.

If you don't focus on what you need to do in order to be successful, how are you going to take care of your family? It really is simple if you let it be.

If you must, buy or rent a small office space and don't "work from home," per se. Make it known what you must do, and if others get upset about it, don't take it personally.

When you are confident, yet soft spoken about setting your boundaries, you are setting an example about how to take care of yourself. You are teaching others some lessons about taking care of themselves, too. Don't wait until you get so frustrated by their interruptions that you explode in anger towards the people around you, because, that isn't professional either. Anger also takes a lot of energy out of you, leaving you unable to concentrate on what you need to do.

Some people say if you are on time, you are late. I used to work at an office where employees had to be there at 7:00 a.m. on the dot. If you weren't there right at 7:00, the door would be locked. People would sit in their cars and cry because they were 10 seconds late and missed out.

Who are they mad at? At the people who told them to be on time, or are they mad at themselves? Some people would say they had to stop and get something to eat. They didn't **have to.** They **chose to** stop and get something to eat. They took a risk, knowing they would probably be late. Or they like to say there was too much traffic; they use that excuse. You live somewhere and work somewhere else-- you know what the traffic is going to be like, so prepare for that and leave extra early.

People will either always rationalize or they just don't care. They are chronically late, and they say they were waiting on such and such to get ready. If you wait for someone like that and are late as a result, then it's your fault, no one told you that you had to wait. If you want to be on time, need to be on time, then leave the other person to their malingering, do what you have to do to get yourself where you have to be—on time! Sometimes you have to send people a hard message. If you don't, they will never get it.

There are a lot of opportunities that are missed because of lateness. People can be late in terms of hours, days, weeks, and months. "You beat 90% of the people, just by showing up." If you just show up, you make yourself available for a lot of things to come your way. If you don't show up on time, you will reap what you sow.

That's the bottom line. A lot of people who show up late ask themselves, "Why didn't I get chosen; what happened?"

They think it's something personal, but that's not it. It is because they were late.

It has nothing to do with if you are highly favored or not, or if you are the best of the best. If you were really the best, you wouldn't be chronically late.

I worked in a field where we gave presentations about business opportunities. Sometimes the guests of these seminars came late and missed the presentation. Afterwards, they wanted me to sit down and go over what they missed with them.

So, what did I do? I told them they had to set up another appointment.

Why? Because, I value my time. If you didn't show up on time, it means that you don't value my time or respect me. So, I'm going to make you wait and set up another time. Doing this is actually a lesson that they need to learn at some point, anyway. It is best that they learn it now. Timeliness is an easy concept to understand, but not so easy to do, especially if you aren't that organized.

Now, if you want to be successful, you need to start valuing your time also. No one is going to take you seriously, if you don't take yourself seriously and are always late. I have done business with people whom I have paid thousands of dollars to work with me. I paid them the money, and they showed up late. That tells me that I should be getting a discount, because I paid for their time, and they didn't show up on time. It was like a slap in the face.

How would you like it if I slapped you in the face? You would be angry, right?

Let's say you work for me. I'm not just paying you for the job I'm paying you for your time. I expect you to be available for the whole time you are getting paid. If you're not there, you can't possibly pay me back for that lost time. I don't want you to give me extra time when we are already over the limit to try and "pay me back." Because that lost time is priceless, and you would be indebted to me forever. I want you to show up on time, that's why I paid you-- for your time. There are consequences to being late and one must realize that God is the only one who can dictate time and get away with it. You may pray for something, but you can't dictate to Him as to when you get what you prayed for. You've heard that saying "God may not come when you want Him to, but He always comes on time." That is the way it works. God is the only one who can dictate time. You cannot disrespect other people and be late and expect to succeed.

I used to work with a lot of people who came late for everything, and they missed out. The first thing they wanted to know was, "What happened, what did I miss?"

They would ask if I recorded the meeting, or presentation. No, I didn't record it, and even if I did I wouldn't give it to them because they should've been there, but they weren't. They missed out. This is their problem not mine.

If you know people like this and give in to them, then they will think that they can always get away with being late. This becomes a matter of respecting yourself and respecting others. Why should you reward them for doing something wrong? That is like giving a present to a child who needed discipline for something that they did wrong. I'm not giving you a gift if you don't show up! Even if you did show up, but were late, I won't give you a present.

Your reward is showing up and not missing out!

If you are one of those people who are always late, shame on you. Even if you have always been that way, if you're going to be successful, you must change, now. It is the only way you are going to succeed in life. Personally,

I think it's funny when people set their alarm clocks early to try and fool themselves, but if that is what will help you, then do it. You could also try going to sleep a little earlier. Prepare your clothes the night before, take a shower the night before, and pack your lunch the night before. It feels great when you wake up and everything is already done, and you probably won't be late, either. Start holding yourself accountable, and if that means kicking your own ass, then do it!

You are a grown man or woman, so follow through on everything you say you are going to do. Follow through on "time." Be a faithful person, and everyone, including me, will know that you can be relied upon. If you tell someone that you are going to be somewhere at a certain time, then be true to your word. Be someone who is honorable and trustworthy. Do you want to be trusted? If you are trustworthy in other people's eyes, then you will be so favored, and blessed beyond compare. This is how you get promotions, raises, and this is how you move forward in the world. If you can't do that, then you have no respect from anyone, and you definitely don't have respect from me. I don't like people who are late.

Many people think that I am overreacting. I bet if you got people to be honest- when you show up late, they will tell you it bothers them, too. When they have to go around asking other people if they have heard from you, there's a problem. When they have to look nervously at their watch while waiting for you instead of enjoying whatever event you're late for, then there's a problem. If someone has to keep calling you, asking if you are still on your way, there's a problem. It's not cute at all. It isn't funny either, but I still laugh at them. I laugh at people who are chronically late, because they are the type of people that don't make it in the world, but still think the world owes them everything on a silver platter.

Many people think it is cool to be late, but it isn't. It isn't o.k. People respect others who are early. This is just in business; I can't speak for others in other areas. But, in business, people respect that. I respect someone who is on time or even early. So, make sure that happens. Put yourself in a position to succeed. How do you do that? Be on time, be early, every time.

I used to belong to a networking group. In the group we were constant sticklers for being on time. We had someone who kept the time, and we always wanted to make sure we were on time. Some people didn't respect that. The network had a way of monitoring timeliness and if someone was late too often, that person was asked to leave.

This is just one example of how being late is detrimental to your success in business. As a member of this group, if you are always late, you may not get the benefits of belonging to the group. This networking group allowed everyone a chance to speak and tell about their business. If you arrive late, you won't be able to do either tell about your business or hear about others, and then you may miss out on referrals for your business from the other people. In the end, it is always your **choice** as to whether you are late or not. If you made the decision not to get up earlier, you chose to be late. Make sure that you are in a position to make things happen for yourself and for your business so that you can succeed.

The moral of the story is: Don't Be Late. Be on time. If this is problematic for you, get in touch with other people who like getting up early, and have them call you as soon as they get up. There are many ways to help yourself. It may feel weird at first, but it will be worth it in the end. No, not everyone is going to be able to be your front-desk-wake-up call, but if you ask around, I'm certain someone will oblige. Many people like getting up before the sun rises. Let them be your inspiration. Let them help you.

Quotes on Lateness

"He was always late on principal. Principal being that punctuality is the thief of time." (Oscar Wilde)

"You cannot do a kindness too soon. For you never know how soon it will be too late." (Ralph Waldo Emerson)

"Everything comes too late for those who wait." (Elbert Hubbard)

By getting up early in the morning, you will have more time at your disposal for work. Scholars get up early to think and contemplate. (Rig Veda)

"Better never than late." (George Bernard Shaw)

"I have noticed that people who are late are often so much jollier than those who have to wait for them." (E.G. Lucas)

There is an immeasurable distance between late and too late. (Og Mandino)

"There is no use doing a kindness if you do it a day too late." *(Charles Kingsley)*

"It's never too late to be who you might have been!" *(George Eliot)*

"Better three hours too soon than a minute too late." *(William Shakespeare)*

"Whilst we deliberate how to begin a thing, it grows too late to begin it." *(Marcus Fabius Quintilian)*

"He that rises late must trot all day." *(Benjamin Franklin)*

"I never knew a man come to greatness or eminence who lay abed late in the morning." *(Jonathan Swift)*

"Apologies are pointless, regrets come too late. What matters is you can move, on you can grow." *(Kelsey Grammer)*

"How does a project get to be a year late? One day at a time. *(Frederick P. Brooks, Jr.)*

"So long as you have courage and a sense of humor, it is never too late to start life afresh." *(Freeman Dyson)*

"It's never too late – never too late to start over, never too late to be happy." *(Jane Fonda)*

A Cautionary Tale – "O"

Oscar was a guy who wanted to play on his high school basketball team. But Oscar was talking to the girls on the day when it was time for tryouts. He was the womanizer of the team because girls love a guy who's great in sports.

Keep in mind; he was one of the best basketball players in school.

The coach didn't play that way; he expected all of his players to be early for practices. When the coach came on the court, he expected everyone to be dressed and ready to go. But here was Oscar, always getting there late, and he thought it was all good, because he wanted to look cool. He was the guy who got all of the girls and could still maintain a good game.

In all reality, he couldn't maintain a good basketball game. He didn't realize that even though the coach let him on the team and let him practice and he was good- he shot the hoops- that when game time came; he always sat at the end of the bench.

He couldn't figure out why, and one day he confronted his coach. Oscar asked his coach, "Why aren't you letting me play, I'm the best player on the team?"

His coach told him "Oscar, you aren't the best player on the team. The best players show up on time, and are there for their teams."

Oscar had to learn that the best players don't let their teams down. They don't put girls first. In putting girls first, Oscar was showing that he didn't care as much about his game or his team.

"Every time you show up late, you not only let yourself down, you let your entire school, and your entire team down," the coach said to Oscar.

So, in the long run, without even realizing it he was letting those girls down, too. The simple moral of this story is: Don't be an Oscar.

Chapter 3 –
Put Me in Coach

We all have imperfections. However, one thing that many people have a problem with is that they are not coachable. They don't want to take instruction from other people. Everyone wants to be in charge and in complete control. Why don't people want to take instructions from others? Because we want to feel secure, confident and like we are in charge, at all times.

Some people have a natural talent to be a leader and only feel good when they are leading. However, the best way to be a great leader is to be humble, teachable, and open-minded. You have to be willing to let other people feel like they are in control. Trust people that they are responsible enough and give them a reason to care about what is going on.

When others feel like they have a stake in something, or are a part of something, they start to "pretend" that it is their own, and when a person feels ownership in a project, or job, or commitment, they take care of it and want to succeed with it. They cannot feel this unless they let go, however.

Anyone reading this book is most likely an adult. As adults, we have grown-up and followed instructions all of our lives. We have grown into free thinkers, and we can make decisions on our own. We feel that our ideas matter, so "I don't need to deal with someone else's ideas."

At this point, sit back and ask yourself a question. You are reading this book because your way didn't work out the way you wanted it to. You tried it your way, and your way didn't seem to work. If you have tried it your way for a while and you keep coming up empty, why don't you try it someone else's way?

Someone once asked, "How do you become a millionaire?"

One answer is to go to lunch with a millionaire, and shut up. Listen to the person who can teach you the things that you want to know, the things that will help you to grow.

You don't always understand what you have to do, and if you aren't open to correction, how are you going to learn the right way to do things?

Are you insecure? Do you need to always be right in order to feel accepted? If you do, then you need to get rid of that mentality in order to succeed in business. Confidence always gets the sale. Remember that.

A case in point is myself: Years ago I worked for a company and my manager would invite me to full-time management meetings. I was only a part-time employee, but she invited me to them, anyway. These meetings were not even during my regular nine to five hours. They were at 11p.m. I sat through these meetings, but I didn't see them as a chore.

It was a learning experience for me. My managers were making the income that I wanted to make, and they were willing to share information with me. So, I said, I need to listen to them, and find out what they want to tell me. They saw something in me, that at the time, I didn't see in myself.

When you are coachable, you look for someone who sees something in you and who can coach you, because they have been there. You may not see ALL the potential in yourself, but they do. If they didn't, they wouldn't waste their time on you.

Would your waste your time on someone who wasn't willing to listen to you? Would you waste your time on someone who continues to argue with you about something you know for certain is right because you've been through it before? Experience is the key. Getting others to understand that the reason they should do things your way is because you have experienced it personally, and it worked for you.

What I also saw was that this person--my manager was selling me on my dreams. I had told them in my interview what I wanted and they took me seriously. They said, "If you want it, here it is, come and get it."

They continued to take me seriously because I was teachable, and I listened. I didn't give them any reason to doubt me.

I didn't ask things like, "Why not do it this way? Or "Why is your way better than my way?"

Some people will just keep going on and argue to the death. It sure feels like death once I'm done listening to someone like that. I don't want someone else doing that to me, so I don't do that to them. I know how it feels when I'm talking to someone who is always ready to say things like, "but" or "well" or even "what if." They are always ready to argue their case, even when they know I'm right. It doesn't make sense.

If the deli ham is going to go bad soon, because it has been sitting in the fridge for two weeks, it is going to go bad. No ifs, ands, or buts about it, right? Imagine someone arguing with you about deli ham, and believing that somehow it will stay good forever. How ridiculous right? They are arguing with you just to argue. It is the same way when a leader tries to lead someone who doesn't follow, even though they have already said that they are going to follow, take the plunge, listen fully, and give up all perceived "control."

It makes me want to move right on to the next person, one who is willing to listen. How about you?

One of the biggest compliments my previous employer gave me later on was, "Barrett is low maintenance. He follows instructions." That is what you want to be, "low maintenance."

If you want to coach and be coached, that is what is required. I didn't require a babysitter. Do you?

If you are depending too much on other people, then you need to grow up, show up, shut up, and listen. Don't talk, just listen and take notes.

You must understand, in order to go where you have never been, you need to find someone who has been there, and be willing to learn how to get there, too. Find someone who has shown others how to get there. This means you have to understand that you need a coach. But, remember, you do not need a babysitter. There is a big difference.

The fact that they need a coach can be a very hard pill for some people to swallow. Let's face it: We all have egos. We all think that we can do things our way, or find another way to go all by ourselves. If you think that your way is "the best way," then at some point you are going to have to understand that your way is not the only way. Your way may work, or it may get you to a certain level. But if your way won't get you all the way to the end, then you need to take that fork in the road that leads to a coach to get to that next level. If you don't, your business will not grow.

There is always another level that you can get to, and someone else may be able to help you get there. Are you human? If so, then you have an ego. All egos are full of pride, so swallow that pride and open your mind. If you can learn to humble yourself and admit that you need help, you will go a very long way in life.

Do you want to go far? Do you want to tread in places that other people only dream of? Don't get stuck in your dream. Instead, turn your dream into reality. You will get stuck if you don't open your mind, and humble yourself.

I'm going to give you another example. This one is about a basketball player named Kobe Bryant. Bryant is one of the best players in his position in the game right now, and he may be for all of history. He also has a coach. I'm not even talking about a team coach; Kobe has a personal trainer. He goes to basketball coaches. He takes his off-season time, and trains with Hall of Fame legends who can teach him new things.

If it is good enough for him, why wouldn't it be good enough for you, if you want to be considered one of the best?

I heard former basketball coach John Thompson who watched Kobe Bryant say, "If the best player in the game took time in his off-season to learn from the best, then why aren't these young guys doing it?"

It goes back to ego again. Some of the younger guys may feel that they have all the athleticism, and all of the talent, in the world. They are healthy, strong, fast, and believe that they can just go with the flow and still make it because of their youth.

This is so far from the truth.

They may say that they don't need anyone else to train them, because they say things like "I know how to play this game, and I'm good."

There is a difference between being good, and being great. The great ones know that they need someone to assist them in getting to that greatness and staying great. If you want to be "good," go right ahead. No one is stopping you.

Yet, you could be stopping yourself from being great. You are also the only one who can let off the brake and decide to step on the gas pedal.

I'm not talking about only basketball; I'm talking about life in general. I'm talking about business, or anything else you want to achieve.

Once you get to a point, you don't stop, you keep going. Take schooling for instance: In order to keep going if you have graduated from high school is to move on to college to get an Associate's Degree, but do you stop there?

You certainly can, many people do. However, if you want to be great, then you will get your Bachelor's, your Master's, and your Doctorate degree. If you have made it to the doctorate level, then to continue on with achieving greatness, start teaching others.

The best way to remember everything you've learned is to teach someone else.

You could also relate this to a promotion at the company you work for. You are going to need someone to be your mentor, someone who can guide you on how to get to your final destination. It could be a spiritual guide even. The sooner you recognize that you need a coach to get you to where you need to be, and want to be, the better off you will be in the end.

However, you have to put aside your ego, and lower your pride. Ego is only a three letter word, but it sure is a long one, and the ego is also very ugly. Ego can get us into so much trouble, because we don't want to swallow our pride and put our ego aside.

I heard the expression, "Check your ego at the door."

We need to listen. God gave us two ears and one mouth, but many of us use our mouth more than our ears. Maybe it is because we are trying to compensate. You have to learn to humble yourself, because if you don't, you will find yourself in a lot of trouble because you aren't listening to what is going on around you. There are a lot of things out there that we need to listen to and learn.

Someone told me that if you have two people who agree on everything, then one of them is not necessary. So, you need to get outside viewpoints, get an opinion from someone who can help you think differently, someone who sees objectively.

This is what a coach does. You need someone to put you in an uncomfortable position where you have never been before. No one else can do this for you quite like a coach can, contrary to what you may be thinking.

Your family and friends, even though you may have thought about them to begin with, will not push you as much as a coach will. If they do, they will let you get away with things. You will never ever be able to learn that way, but a coach is going to push you to the point of painful and uncomfortable feelings.

No pain, no gain, right?

This uncomfortable feeling is always going to make you feel strange, and maybe even weak. You have to decide if this uncomfortable feeling is worth it to become successful. Are you willing to buck up, shut up, and listen up for once?

At first, you are going to try to fight against it with your ego by defending yourself, because, this is a natural response. Always remember, this is just a feeling. You can't live by your feelings your entire life. If you do, then maybe you aren't cut out for business. If you feel the need to be comfortable at all times, then you aren't going to be successful. Success and comfort do not mix. You are going to be hearing that a lot.

Do you want to learn to be a millionaire? Like I said earlier, take one out to lunch and listen. This isn't just for becoming a millionaire. If you want to learn to be the best, take the person who is the best out to lunch, and learn to listen. Keep your mouth shut, and listen, listen, listen. Retain everything you hear by shutting up, taking notes and listening.

Most coaches have a certain system. In that system, they want to make sure that you can follow it, and they can transfer it to you. One of my mentors once told me, "It doesn't matter what works, it matters what can be duplicated." If you can't duplicate that system, then it isn't much of a system to begin with. You need to follow some sort of system.

If you notice, when going to a personal trainer to work out, your trainer has a system they want you to follow. They meet you where you are with your diet, your physique, capacity, how hard they work you out, and even when you need to take a break. This system will eventually be turned up to the next level, once you make it through this first level. It's like a Mario Brothers game where you keep leveling-up.

Let's go back to basketball for another example. One of the greatest coaches in basketball was named Phil Jackson. Phil Jackson coached Michael Jordan to six N.B.A. championships. He also coached Kobe Bryant to five N.B.A. championships.

I think it is safe to say that Phil Jackson knows how to coach. He has a system, and he used the same system with Kobe Bryant and Shaquille O'Neil. He also used this system with both Scottie Pippen and Michael Jordan. Different players, different teams, same system, same results, and because of that, they won. He is known as a legend. His system made him into someone that all of these basketball players respected. Because they respected him, they would have run through a wall for him, and they will even tell you that.

They realized that what he was telling them would propel them to a level of play that they had never been at before. Now they were going to be at a higher echelon than the rest of their peers. Their team would also be at a higher echelon than their opponents. The Chicago Bulls won the NBA title under Phil Jackson's tutelage and set a record season for wins that no other team has ever come close to before. That is because they followed the system. If a coach has a system for you to follow, then you need to follow that system and make it work for you. The system should be easily duplicate-able. That does not mean the work won't be difficult or challenging. But the system should be something that many can follow to achieve a desired result. If it is not something you can follow, you may need to look for another system.

Here is another example in sports. Mike Tomlin, who is a football coach for the Pittsburgh Steelers, followed a legend, who himself, had followed a legend. The 1st legend was named Chuck Knoll. He was the coach for the Steelers who won four Super Bowls. He was followed by Bill Cowher, who brought an attitude to that team. That team wanted to follow him and they loved him. He won a Super Bowl with the team, also.

Now, here comes Mike Tomlin. He was a man with no previous head coaching experience. It was very odd for the Pittsburgh Steelers to hire him, because he was an African American coach, and that wasn't a prevailing theme in the league at that time. Mike Tomlin knew he had some battles to fight to get the respect he wanted. When Bill Cowher left, Tomlin knew he had some big shoes to fill. To be successful, he had to implement his system. He made things uncomfortable for the players. The players didn't like him, but he had to let the team know that he was now in charge. Bill Cowher was gone and not coming back.

Tomlin had to make the players follow his system. So, what did he do? Normally, when veteran players come out for a new season, they get a little less playing time and practice time than the new players get. . Tomlin had all of the players come in at the same time, and made them all work just as hard together. He worked the veteran players just as much as he worked those younger guys.

The veterans wondered why he was so rough on them, because Tomlin was killing them! They thought he was crazy, but he was only making a point. He was proving his point to get them to buy into his system.

It was kind of rough, and there were some really hard times, and there were many ups and downs the first year. Tomlin had a hard-nosed approach like Bill Cowher. So, the players started adopting that hard-nosed approach, also. In adopting that approach, they started winning games.

In Tomlin's second year, as head coach for the Steelers, they won the Super Bowl. They had bought into their coach's system.

If your coach doesn't have a system, you need to find another coach. You are always going to need a coach.

So, let's talk about you-- being coachable. This is one of the biggest, most important areas that we need to talk about. Let's talk about what you need to be coachable. Are you coachable? Are you willing to fight? Can you change? Are you willing to change? Will you commit to change? Can you handle the pain of change? It is going to be painful, but in the end, it will be highly rewarding. There is a big difference between being willing to change, and actually making the commitment to do so.

Most people will say that they are going to change, but only a few will commit to it. This means you can't just give up when things get difficult. It's going to get worse before it gets better, because while you are in the middle of having those familiar layers of habit peeled off, it's going to hurt. Changing behavior is like taking skin off a horse's back. You are opening up and laying yourself completely bare emotionally when going through change. It hurts like hell, but after all is said and done, it feels like heaven.

You have to say, "You know what, no matter what comes my way, I'm going to keep at it, and I'm going to make sure I become a better, productive, different, person, and I want to become a person that other people admire and respect."

You need to know that about yourself, that you can make that type of commitment and keep it for the long haul.

I'll use for example the desire and dedication to lose weight. Many people say they are going to do it, and feel brand new before they even start because of their motivation. New goals feel great when you talk about them.

However, when you actually start walking toward your goal, it becomes a struggle, and you have to fight against yourself sometimes. To lose weight, you have to change your diet; you can't eat cupcakes and pizzas all day long. The change must be long term, too. If you stop eating junk food and fast food for a month, you may lose a little, but if you start eating that stuff again the very next month, you will gain all the weight back, and then some.

You need to be honest about yourself if you want to make a goal to change. You need to say, "I do have flaws, I do have faults, and I need to get a grasp of them all, and change those things."

You usually can't change unless you acknowledge every area of weakness that you have. That's how it goes with dieting. You usually cannot lose weight, and look good if you continue to eat junk food, sugary items, and fattening foods. If it is a matter of you not being able to show up on time at meetings, then you need to change that. If you don't, then you aren't going to be able to get where you need to be.

Change that about yourself. Do you think you can do it? I dare you to try. Most of you probably won't make it to the end. People have such a hard time finishing things. If you do want to make it, then listen to what I'm saying:

Don't be critical of people who offer you a different perspective. There is more than one way to look at things. You've heard the saying, "There is more than one way to skin a cat."

Well, this is the same thing. There are many other things out there to help you, but you just haven't thought of them. Maybe someone else has, and they are trying to lead you in the right direction. Some people may come to you with one of these alternative approaches, so don't get crazy and hostile. Be humble, and realize that they have nothing against you, personally.

If someone comes to you with a different approach, is it going to kill you to give it a try? An "Oh my gosh, I'm going to die!" type of attitude will paralyze you. So, if you find yourself in a shocked state of mind, accept it, and change your thoughts. This is where will-power may come in handy. Changing your thoughts to a positive stance about being coached is one of the most powerful things that you can do. It changes your emotions, and hence, your actions.

You'd be surprised at what may work for you if you had someone else to guide you. Don't be critical of those who want to help. You've heard the saying, "What doesn't kill you only makes you stronger," right?

Do you want to be stronger and better? If so, then let your old self die. Kill the old ways, attitudes, and actions, and resurrect yourself into a new life. It is going to be a battle; it is going to be hell, but let other people help you along, and admit what it is that needs to be changed.

People love to help others, people love to encourage and see others grow, develop, and change. It is like watching a caterpillar turn into a butterfly. At first, all they see is an ugly worm. Get that ugliness out of you. If you feel the need, let them know the truth - that you are going through growing pains. If they are worthy of you, not only will they understand completely, but they will perceive these growing pains as something they have also experienced.

Tell them that you are in the process of changing over from old bad habits to new good ones, and that you need their help and patience. If you are patient, in the end, you will spread your wings and soar, while showing off your "new, true colors."

Has anyone ever said something to you like, "You are showing your true colors when you act like that?"

Guess what? You don't have to keep those colors; they can be changed, if you are willing to gain those that are much brighter.

Are you willing to go through the hard transformation from being a caterpillar to a beautiful butterfly, knowing ahead of time that you are going to feel ugly, and other people may see your ugliness emerge even more while you are changing? Look at the cocoon, from which the butterfly emerges. That's quite an ugly shell in itself.

This is not just for one area in life, either. This is in all areas of life, and that's why you need a coach. Even if no one else is there to help you, and be patient with the insanity that will show through while you are changing, your coach will be there, and he or she will completely understand.

Maybe you need some "constructive criticism." Don't take it as "destructive" criticism, even though it should be called that, because, it is meant to destroy who you used to be. Whatever you call it, don't just take it with a grain of salt; take the criticism with some pepper, sautéed onions, and add a little butter on the side. Take the constructive criticism and build upon it, because in order to "build up," you must first destroy the rubble and rock that lay there.

Constructive criticism should help you grow, so take it, use it, and let it make you stronger, and better. You have to be open to it. If you aren't open to it, then you will see it in a totally different way than it was originally meant. If you see it in a wrong way, you are hurting yourself. You aren't hurting the person who gave you the constructive criticism.

If you aren't open to constructive criticism, you are going to see it in a completely different way; you are going to feel rejected. You will then focus on the pain of the so-called "rejection" instead of realizing that someone is trying to help you, not hurt you.

There was a gentleman that I used to do business with, and he had a hard time taking constructive criticism. Every time someone said, "It might be a good idea if you tried this," he would respond with, "Yeah, but..." He didn't want to open himself to listening to other people's opinions, so it held him back. Eventually, however, he made a change.

Once he started opening up to people around him and the wealth of knowledge they shared, his business started growing. He eventually got to a level that everyone around him knew he could get to, even though he hadn't seen it. The basic premise here is that he was being pessimistic, and everyone else was being optimistic. Once he started to realize that others could truly help him, he started listening to everyone around him. He opened his mind to what they were saying, and he started taking action. His business then blew up to the sky and he continued to excel.

But, that is what happens in business. You have to open yourself up to the information of people who are around you. You can't know everything- no one can. Understanding and accepting the fact that you will never know everything will help you to be more humble. You may actually feel relieved of the delusional thought that you are supposed to know everything and always be in control. It may lift the excessive weight that you carry around everywhere you go off your shoulders. You will realize that you don't have to carry it at all, and others will gladly help carry it for you if you will let them.

One of the greatest examples I can give you is about Magic Johnson, who was an all-star Los Angeles Lakers basketball player. He could lead a team on his own. He won five N.B.A championships, three Most Valuable Player awards, and three playoff's Most Valuable Player awards. But the one thing he hadn't tackled was the business world.

Once he retired from basketball, he decided to get into the business world. It had always been a dream of his. Being a competitive person, and a coachable person, he had it in him to become an entrepreneur. Magic Johnson felt the pull to learn more about becoming a business owner. He always knew he had he had a "gift," but had never explored it. He needed some advice in order to help bring out his leadership ability.

So, in deciding to explore his leadership abilities, and entrepreneurship inherent within his own personality, he knew he had to do a few things first. He knew he had a lot to learn yet. He challenged himself to learn how to be a successful business person. What do you think he did? He met with people who knew things that he didn't yet know. He went to some of the top business minds and asked them to teach him how to be successful in business. Once he did that, they were all on board because they realized this man who had already achieved so much in his life: fame, fortune, respect, you name it, was humbling himself.

He was there saying, 'You know more than I do, so I need to learn from you.'

Instead of just buying a business and putting his name on it and making it famous, Magic and his "business coaches" took a different approach. When other athletes or famous people have bought a business and put their name on it, historically speaking, those businesses haven't survived long because a "name" alone, doesn't guarantee success.

Johnson's coaches wanted him to take a different approach. They told Magic to find some of the top businesses out there like Starbucks, T.G.I.Friday's, A.M.C. Theatres, and put his name on those.

He still had the fame of his name to draw people in, but he also had an already established and successful business. They were all running well before he came along, so right away he was able to make money and so were the companies. Right now, Magic Johnson is one of the biggest business moguls going today and he was coachable enough to listen to other people. If you open yourself up, the coaching will open up for you, too.

We talked about being a coach and being coachable. You need to ask yourself: "Am I willing to try new things?" If you can answer yes, then you are on your way. Some people are so close-minded that they aren't willing to say, "Yes." You also need to be able to listen to someone who gives you advice, without rebuttal or comment. Saying, "that won't work because," is counterproductive. Just listen, instead. Their ideas may propel you on to creating even newer, better ideas.

Another thing you need to do is respect the coach. Don't get me wrong, respect is something that is earned, but you have chosen your coach. If you 'dis' your coach, you are 'dissing' yourself. If the coach has shown someone else the way to go and has been there before and helped others like you, then there is nothing to question. You need to show this person respect.

You also need to be able to have "blind faith." A lot of people think I may be getting spiritual. Well, maybe I am. If you have blind faith in your spirituality, then you need some blind faith for the person you are bringing on as a coach.

Consider this: Our first coaches in life are our parents. We have blind faith in our parents. We just trust that our parents are going to be there for us. It is blind faith, and you need this faith in your coach. The coach's job is to make you a better person, and if they don't then they will ruin their own reputation as a coach.

You need to have blind faith in your coach. If you constantly challenge your coach, you will end up in a position that isn't going to help you win, and you aren't going to make it. You are designed to compete, but only with other businesses. Don't compete with your manager or your trainer, because it is like you are competing with yourself.

Have you heard the saying, "Don't bite the hand that feeds you"? It is metaphorically the same idea. If you challenge the one who is helping you become a better person, you are essentially telling him or her that no matter what they say, even if it sounds good, you are still going to do things your own way. What is the point of even having a coach, then?

You also need to be able to look in the mirror and tell yourself, "I need to improve this, and I need to improve that." Anyone who looks in the mirror and thinks that they are perfect in every way obviously has many flaws. Anyone who can look in the mirror, honestly, will realize and admit that they have different things that need improvement. By working on those things, you will make yourself better. If you don't, you will always be flawed.

Another thing to work on is showing up on time. You've heard people say, "When the student is ready, the teacher will appear." It is also the other way around. "When the teacher is ready, the student will appear." That is, the student must show up.

You need to show up when the coach is ready to coach you. If you don't, then you've lost the game before it started. You have already shown that you are not coachable. If the coach says to be there at 8:00, then show up at 7:30.

There was a gentleman that was supposed to go on a trip with me and we had to leave early in the morning. I told him to show up at 5:30a.m. He showed up at 6:15, and I was gone. He wasn't being coachable.

Coach-ability is a big issue, and to be a part of that, you need to show up. You also need to be excited about your change. Excitement is contagious. It doesn't matter what you are trying to do in life, you need to be truly excited in order to obtain motivation. If you want to continue to be motivated, and dedicated, then you need to discipline yourself. No one is going to discipline you. No one is going to force you to do anything in this life. Be truly excited and joyful, if you are trying to become a better:

- Student
- Leader
- Parent
- Spouse
- Producer
- Salesman
- Athlete

You need to get excited, because that excitement is going to drive you on those days that you don't want to get out of bed. You need to be excited about the end result, but you also need to keep your excitement flowing during the journey. Life isn't about the final destination; it is about the path you take to get there. Your path can be very different, if you let it. The only way to do this is to maintain your excitement and do whatever you can to keep it going.

Thomas Luebbe, a soccer coach once said, "Having a great game is not the result of spontaneous combustion. You have to light yourself on fire." You need to do whatever you can to access that passion and excitement. Write your goals down, think about your dreams often, and share them with someone. If you know why you have to get up every day, you are going to want to get up early no matter what the cost.

Be willing to sacrifice, also. Sacrifice is very hard. Especially when dieting and working out. You have to make yourself uncomfortable and wake up early to work out. You have to push away the cupcakes, cookies, sodas, and pizza. Start eating food that is good for you, take supplements, and vitamins so that your body will react well. Try new healthy recipes. Find some healthy restaurants that only use organic food. You cannot do the things you used to do that made you comfortable. Give up things you would normally partake in.

You also need to be honest with yourself. Say, "I'm on track," or "I'm so far behind," or "I'm not being coachable."

But first, you have to be honest and say, "I need a coach."

You also have to be honest with your coach. Many people don't want to be honest with their coach. I'm a coach, and I can tell when someone is not being honest with me. If you aren't being honest with yourself it shows in your results. You know that expression, "Actions speak louder than words." This is so true when you are working and in how you conduct yourself; your actions will show through.

You also need to be a team player. Sometimes, it isn't just about you improving. It is about an entire team or unit getting better. You are a part of that team, so you must perform at the optimal level. Your coach can make you someone that can be the leader for the team. You don't need a title to be a leader. You lead mainly by your actions and efforts. You can lead from any position as long as you do your job, and do it well. But you must be a team player if you want to be a leader.

You also don't want to pass the blame. If your coach criticizes you to help you improve, don't pass the buck to someone else. Take it like an adult. Take the responsibility and say, "You know what coach, you're right, I'm responsible for this. I admit I was wrong. Is there anything that you can tell me to help me improve?"

The last area I want to talk to you about is being ready to spend money on coaching. This is an uncomfortable area, but if you want to get better, coaching usually doesn't come for free. You don't have to pay an arm and a leg, but you need to be ready to spend some money. If someone is going to help you learn how to get better, isn't it worth spending the money? Coaching is an investment of money, and time. Coaches spend their precious time to encourage you and help you grow and change. Don't let cost deter you. Success is priceless.

Quotes on Coaching

"Coaching is a profession of love. You can't coach people unless you love them." (Eddie Robinson)

"I don't believe in team motivation. I believe in getting a team prepared so it knows it will have the necessary confidence when it steps on a field and be prepared to play a good game." (Tom Landry)

"Coaching is an action, not a title, and actions result in successes!" (Byron and Catherine Pulsifer)

"Who exactly seeks out a coach? Winners who want more out of life. (Chicago Tribune)

"I absolutely believe that people, unless coached, never reach their maximum capabilities." (Bob Nardelli, former CEO, Home Depot)

"In a recent study, training improved leadership skills by 22%. When combined with executive coaching, improvement jumps to 77%." (Fortune)

"One of the most important tasks of a manager is to eliminate his people's excuses for failure." (Robert Townsend)

"A coach is someone who can give correction without causing resentment." (John Wooden)

"A coach's greatest asset is his sense of responsibility – the reliance placed on him by his players." (Knute Rockne)

"'How' is a great thing to know. 'Why' is the ultimate. I'm the 'why' coach. Why are we doing this? Why are we not doing that? Why is this not working? Those are the things I want to know." (Mike Singletary)

"You want your coach's blessing." (Candace Parker)

A Cautionary Tale – "M"

This tale is about Michael who wanted to be a leader. He had so many ideas of being a leader in his company. He saw other leaders around him, and he thought he could be better than them. He thought he could open up his own branch, but he just needed the opportunity.

So, he was given the opportunity. He took care of his own management team, and he was doing pretty well, but some areas needed improvement. The main area was his own coach-ability.

When some of the higher-ups in the company wanted to show Michael how to do things a little better, he admitted that their ideas were good, but he still insisted upon doing things "his way." The higher-ups said to Michael, "You know, I think you have the right idea, but **this** approach will work better for you." Michael didn't want to change. He became very stubborn.

Michael insisted on going his own route, because he had his own ideas that he really believed were the best. He thought all he needed to do was give them a little more time.

Gradually, he ended up losing the people who were following him because they weren't seeing any other growth. Michael couldn't see from the out-side- in. None of us can.

Ultimately, Michael was using the leaders in his own manipulative way, and in the end, he was demoted and his income started shrinking. The moral of the story: Listen to your coaches; they can help you get to another level.

Don't be a Michael.

Chapter 4 –
Fruits of Passion

Have you ever been in love? Have you a felt so strongly about someone, in a way you have never felt before, or in a way that made you believe you would do anything for them? Would you give your life for them, do odd things for them, maybe things that are totally out of character, defend that person until the very end, or even go through a wall for them, if necessary. That's what they call passion, where you lose all control and would lay your life down for a person.

My question is, if you had that same type of feeling when it came to your goals, your business, your desires in life, would you do something about it? Do you have a passion? Is there something that you will fight for until the end? You need to have something you are always striving for in life. That's what this chapter is about.

What is passion?

Let's go to the dictionary:

Any powerful or compelling emotion or feeling, like love or hate. Strong amorous feeling or desire; love ardor. Strong sexual desire or lust. An instance or experience of strong love or sexual desire. A person to whom one feels strong love or sexual desire. An extravagant or strong fondness, enthusiasm, or desire for anything: music for example. Passion is "An outburst of strong emotion or feelings, or violent anger." The state of being acted upon or being affected by something external, especially something that is opposite to one's nature; you can be passionate about your theology.

There are a lot of things you can be passionate about.

What is your passion? Can you pinpoint it? Your loved ones may be your passion, but you can't sit around looking at them all day. So, in order to satisfy your passion you need to channel it into or toward something else. If you have a passion for something other than a person, that is even better. You want to make sure that you have something that you are working toward, something that you can fight for, something no one else can deter you from. That is what your passion needs to be.

Do you have it? I don't know.

Is it something you can grasp? No, not physically.

Your passion has to be something that burns inside you, that motivates you, that pushes you, and drives you on a daily basis. It has to be something that keeps you up at night, and gets you up early in the morning because you know that that's what's going to get you where you need to be.

I know some people feel that way about a certain person, activity, sport, or business. You may work very hard at your business, and I'm that way: Business is my passion. People are always saying I am always focused on my business, and I work very hard. To me, it doesn't feel like work, because it is my passion and I love it. I would do it for free because it is my passion and I enjoy it

A passion is something you enjoy with all of your heart. Some of you reading this book feel that way about your activities or sports. Some of you will get up and work harder than the other person. Some people feel that way about their music. It keeps them going. Without that passion they may feel empty inside.

If you don't feel it, you need to find it. You need to sit down and ask yourself, "What is it that I love to do?"

When I say that, it makes me sad, because most people in this world are working for something that they have no real passion for. Most people in this world get up early in the morning, before the sun comes up, and get the morning cup of caffeine nerves (coffee), put that in their system and get ready for the day.

Let's talk more about passion and what you are willing to do. If you are passionate about your work, it will show. I don't see my work as "work." I see it as something I get up and do every day, and I'm excited about doing it. Do you have that same passion, desire, and zeal? Is there anything inside of you that pushes you to do your work? If you don't have that passion, you need to find a passion. You need to find what drives you. What makes you excited? It may seem trivial to you right now, and you may be telling yourself, "That's nothing to be passionate about."

I'll give you an example. When I was in college, I started out as an architecture major. Architecture kicked my butt; I'm not going to lie to you. I was working late at night on projects, and getting four hours of sleep. My grades were bad, and I knew I had to change my major. I knew I couldn't do this as a career. I knew if I was doing this bad in my freshman year, it was only going to get harder.

I couldn't decide what I was going to change my major to, however. Then my sister called me one night, and I started pouring out my heart, telling her my dilemma of not knowing what I wanted to do with my life and what I should major in.

She said, "Well maybe you should major in television broadcasting or radio, you've always liked that kind of stuff."

The first thing I thought was, "Well, who would major in that? Everyone likes television. That's not a major, who can't do that."

She talked me into giving it a shot, because she knew it was something I had always been passionate about, but I hadn't seen it as something that I could do as a career.

So, I changed my major to Mass Media Arts, because it had always been my passion. I was on the dean's list every semester. I ended up writing for the school newspaper, and hosted television shows for the post football and basketball teams. I ended up being the sports director for the campus radio station. When I did that, everyone around me saw that I was passionate about it, to the point that I was jokingly dubbed, "Mr. Mass Media."

I was also known around the campus as the person who called the games on the radio. It was so much fun to me. Others may have seen it as a chore, but

I saw it as something fun. I didn't recognize it as a passion at first, because I didn't take it as seriously as others did.

This may be the same for you. You may not see your passion as something that drives you right now. It may be something that excites you, or that you deem as fun, or something that interests you. But when you put it in the context of a career, or something that you will do every day, then it will drive you like a passion.

Another example of a passion is something that drives you to help people. I was approached by several different business entities. A lot of them were network marketing companies. One of the things that got me is the company I'm affiliated with called, "Metro Public Adjustment." They are a company that assists homeowners and business owners with insurance claim settlements. Before they assist a customer with an insurance claim settlement, they educate them about their policy.

If you are like most homeowners, you have no idea what is in your insurance policy. You get the policy because you have to have it, and you move on. The only time most people know anything about what is in their policy is the day they buy it, or when something happens to their property, and it is too late. Metro educates you about what's in your policy, so if something happens it won't be too late for you. They also represent the client to make sure that if they have a claim, the insurance company will pay them fairly, and they help them to maximize that settlement.

When I saw that, I said, "I could get passionate about this." With my background of working in insurance and real estate, I didn't know much about this very important area, and I should have known about it. I realized if I didn't know this, how many other people out there didn't have this information. That is when I became passionate about it and become a part of this company, because I wanted to help others who didn't know about it, either.

My passion has driven me to succeed, and I was recognized as a leader in the company. I also helped a lot of people in the process. You don't know how much of a thrill it is for someone to say to me, "Thank you so much, I didn't have this information, and you have helped me so much." It is a thrill to hear that from the people I'm helping, and I cannot tell you what it feels like. But, if you find your passion and you work your passion, you will get that same feeling because it makes you feel good to know that you can do something you love and others can benefit from it, as well.

You have to be excited about your passion, and get up in the morning focused on it. You want to hear people comment about how happy they see you are. When others say, "Wow, I like the way John is doing that business, because you can see his excitement and happiness." That is when you know you have found your passion. You need to do things that complement your passion.

People can compliment you, but you must do the things that complement your passion. It could be things as simple as, if your passion is to open up your own restaurant, then start cooking, catering, or even begin writing a blog about restaurants. Do things that complement your passion. You will be surprised at what happens.

Have you ever written down your passion? Have you ever taken the time to write down – "This is what I'm going to do; this is how I'm going to do it, and how I'm going to start"? Maybe you need to create a business plan of sorts to get connected with your passion.

My belief is that your passion is right there inside you, but if you don't write it down how will God ever know you are truly serious? God already knows what is inside of you, because He put it there! He wants to see if you are really serious about pursuing it, because He put that passion inside of you. If you squash it, ignore it, and don't go after it, you will lose it. Someone else will rise up and take your place. However, if you stop procrastinating, write it down, tell Him about it, and start moving toward it, God will make a way at just the right place and right time for you to finally start on this amazing life-long journey of fulfilling your dreams.

The most difficult part is beginning. If you just take that leap of faith, no matter what you see, or what you don't have available, God will provide what you need, but only after you take the first step, not before. How can He provide you with something if you don't let him know that you are ready?

Compare God to a banker. God owns everything that we see and don't see. If you need a business loan, you must show the banker your plans. If you don't, it is unlikely that he will loan you any money; he is going to think you are crazy and you might just blow all of the money. However, if you have a clear plan, and you write it down and explain it all to the banker (God), then he will more than likely give you a loan. No matter how you look at it, God isn't going to just give or loan you money, but you still have to present your ideas to God so that He will give you what you need to move forward with your dreams.

Do you associate with other passionate people, or do you deal with people who want to work their rut every day and never go after their passion? If the latter is true, you will never achieve your passion, because others will always keep you at their level. Deal with people who are really passionate, even if their passion is about something completely different from yours. Get that synergy going between the two of you, because when you do, you will be amazed at what can happen.

Let's talk again about the normal rut of life. Do you want to deal with people who work their rut from nine to five, and never do anything? Many people get up in the morning when it is still dark outside, and they cannot see a thing. The devil made alarm clocks. God gets me up when He wants to get me up, and usually the sun is up so I can actually see what I'm doing, and I get up with a passion for my day.

We drink the morning cup of nerves, then we go outside and start up our cars so that they will warm up a little bit, and then we go back inside and watch a little news. Maybe we eat something, and then we are off to the races. We head out to work and chase taillights, sucking in exhaust fumes, on our way to a place we don't want to be.

We don't necessarily even like the people we work with; we would never invite them to our homes, and we wouldn't want to spend any more time with them than we have to.

We work for a bunch of people who want us to check in at a certain time, tell us when to go on break, how long we can stay on break, when to go to lunch, and even when to go to the bathroom. We leave at a certain time, and when we are headed home, sometimes we leave and it is dark, yet again.

So, we spend all of our daylight hours at place where we don't want to be. We start chasing taillights again, suck in some more exhaust fumes, get home, maybe cook dinner or clean, which is even more work. Help the kids with their homework and other childlike issues. Then if we're lucky we get to sit down and breathe for a minute, watch a favorite television show, then go to bed, just to get up and do it, again.

Some of us do that for 40 years.

Then after 40 years of the same stuff, we retire. I don't know if they should call it "retire" because a person is just "tired." That stuff just wears a person out.

That is why I call it the rut of life.

You spend your whole life not going after your passion. You spend your whole life dreaming about something but you never pursue it. Your passion is what makes your pursuit. Have a passionate pursuit. You have to go after it, fight for it, and go through anything to get there. You have to ask yourself some questions, and you also have to answer them honestly. Let that passion burn within you until you are so on fire that you light everyone else around you on fire, too.

Quotes About Passion

"At the end of the day, we all need to remember to keep going. However, just making it another day doesn't get us where we truly want to be. We must move with vigor, passion, and a fixed determination to achieve our goals." (Khalil Gibran, Artist)

"The only people for me are the mad ones. The ones who are mad to live, mad to talk, to be saved, desirous of everything at the same time. The ones who never yawn, or say commonplace things, but burn, burn, burn like fabulous yellow Roman candles exploding like spiders across the stars and in the middle and you see the blue center light pop and everybody goes, "Awww." (Jack Peroack)

"A person can succeed at almost anything for which they have almost unlimited enthusiasm." (Charles Schwab)

"I have no special talents, and only passionately curious." (Albert Einstein)

"Passion, it lies in all of us, sleeping, waiting, and though unwanted, unbidden, it will stir, open its jaws and howl; it speaks to us, guides us; passion rules us all, and we obey. What other choice do we have? Passion is the source of our finest moments, the joy of love, the clarity of hatred, and the ecstasy of grief. It hurts sometimes more than we can bear. If we could live without passion, maybe we would know some kind of peace. But we would be hollow, empty rooms shuttered and dank. Without passion we'd truly be dead. (Josh Weeden)

"A great leader's courage to fulfill his vision comes from passion, not position." (John Maxwell)

"Courage is going from failure to failure without losing enthusiasm." (Winston Churchill)

"There is no end, there is no beginning. There is only the passion of life." (Fredercico Felini)

"Nothing great in the world has been accomplished without passion." (George Wilham, Frederick Heigl)

"Rest and reason rule in passion." (Kalil Gebron)

"Passion is the Genesis of genius." (Anthony Robbins)

"If passion drives you, let reason hold the reins." (Benjamin Franklin)

"Renew your passion daily." (Terry Metz)

"You want to make sure you are passionate about everything that moves you, whatever excites you, and whatever it is that makes you happy, you need to be passionate about it. (Unknown)

"The most powerful weapon on earth is the human soul on fire." (Ferdinand Foch)

"If there is no passion in your life then have you really lived? Find your passion, whatever it may be. Become it and let it become you and you will find great things happen for you, to you, and because of you." (T. Alan Armstrong, Writer and Author)

"Enthusiasm is one of the most powerful engines of success. When you do a thing, do it with all your might. Put your whole soul into it. Stamp it with your own personality. Be active be energetic and faithful, and you will accomplish your object. Nothing great was ever achieved without enthusiasm." (Ralph Waldo Emerson)

"When you set yourself on fire, people love to come and see you burn." (John Wesley)

"Purpose may point you in the right direction, but it's passion that propels you." (Travis McAshan)

"Enthusiasm is nothing more or less than faith in action." (Henry Chester)

"Passion and purpose go hand in hand. When you discover your purpose, you will normally find it's something you're tremendously passionate about." (Steve Pavlina)

"One person with passion is better than 40 people merely interested." (E.M. Forster)

"My fault, my failure, is not in the passions I have, but in my lack of control of them." (Jack Kerouac)

"I'm already crazy. I'm a fearless person. I think it creeps up on you. I don't think it can be stopped. If my destiny is to lose my mind because of fame, then that's my destiny. But my passion still means more than anything." (Lady Gaga)

"Those who danced were thought to be quite insane by those who could not hear the music." (Angela Monet)

A Cautionary Tale – "O"

Olivia is a very talented musician. She can sing like no other, play keyboard, guitar, and she can even act. When she was in school she was in every play, and did extremely well. She also wrote songs, played and produced music; she did everything. But Olivia had reservations about whether she could be great, and she never actively pursued her passion.

She would listen to music; she would stay in her studio in her own home. She never let anyone hear her music, so no one else could hear how great she was.

Oddly enough, Olivia had a friend, who wasn't quite as talented, but she could sing. This person went on to record a C.D., and it made her millions of dollars. Olivia had to sit back and watch regretfully, because she had never pursued her passion.

Don't be an Olivia.

Chapter 5 –
Nobody's Perfect

Perfectionism is a deadly word, but even more so, it is a deadly way of life. A perfectionist is a person who never seems to be happy with the way things go, because they have to make sure everything is perfect first. Everything has to be "right," and they cannot move forward until it is right. They say things like, "There is always this holding me up" or "This is keeping me back," or "I can't do it until I get everything in place."

The truth is, nothing will ever be completely in place. If you wait until it is, then you will be waiting forever.

Nobody is perfect, and your plans are not going to happen the way you always envisioned them. You can hire the best and the brightest; you can wait for that perfect moment. It just isn't going to come.

Unfortunately, the perfectionist is always thinking this way. They miss out on opportunities, because they are still trying to get everything perfect. They can't seem to figure it out, even though they have it figured out.

Are you one of these people who never do anything, because not everything is going according to plan?

Sometimes plans must change. Usually, when they do, they change for the best, but the problem is, perfectionists cannot see that "best" yet. Maybe, the finished product isn't meant for you to see until the end. If you were able to see everything now, then it may change again and again and again.

When we make plans, the end result is our best guess according to our capabilities. It's like science, and we just have to believe that at every moment we are doing the best we can do for who we are, what we know, and what we've learned.

I was like that years ago. I told people that I was going to move to Atlanta. The problem was, I held up three years of my life trying to perfect things before I actually moved. I kept telling people, "I'm going to move when I get this right" or "When I get this amount of money together, I'm moving." It took me three years to realize that everything doesn't happen the way I wanted it to happen or when I wanted it to happen. Three years to realize that I was not going to get everything right, right on time.

Once you get those things in line, you'll think of other things that you have to do and the delay will continue. Instead of thinking everything has to be 'perfect' before doing something, just step out and do it. Once you step out in faith, you will be surprised at your results. You'll realize that you don't control things. You are not in control. God is the only one who is in control in this life, and you can't take on that responsibility. He is the only one who is allowed to be perfect. We are supposed to shoot for excellence.

So, take the pressure off yourself, and stop telling yourself things have to be perfect. Things don't have to be perfect. The sooner off you realize that, the better off you will be. You have to get in the place of mind where you say to yourself, "You know what, things aren't going to be perfect, but I can still do this, and I'm going to do it." Until you do that you are always going to be held up by procrastination, and you will never get to where you want to be in life.

Perfection and striving-to-be-the-best are two totally different things. A lot of you are perfectionists. If you are a perfectionist because you are an Achiever, that means you strive for perfection because you always win and you are always at the top, and you continue moving toward another level. That is a good attitude to have because you won't stay stagnant, and it is different than being a perfectionist who holds himself back. If you stay stagnant after achieving something, you will be extremely bored, and you won't grow anymore.

Let me give you an example of "good" perfectionism: Michael Jordan and basketball.

Jordan was a perfectionist and he hating losing. He hated losing no matter what he was doing in life. No one likes to lose; we all can admit that, but Jordan would always strive to be the best. He was an achiever, a winner. He put himself in a position to win because he worked at it and didn't sit back and procrastinate.

The perfectionist will say, "I'm not going on the basketball court unless my shoe laces are right" or "I'm not going on the basketball court until they give me a different ball." Those little things are what hold you back. It's never going to happen that everything is perfect.

Consider the "Do or Die" person versus the person who learns from their mistakes. The "Do or Die" person says, "If it doesn't turn out this way, then forget it."

The "Do or Die" person says, "If I don't get it the way I want it, it's over; I'm not going to do it."

It's if they don't "do" what they had planned, then they will "die" from trying. It's as if they KNOW it won't work, or they will die from apathy or giving up completely.

When keeping a rigid perfectionistic attitude it doesn't matter how many plans you make or new projects you venture out on, you will fail every single time.

A lot of people think like that. Many will say, "I'm not going to pursue my dreams until this is in place, or this is lined up first." Or "I'm no longer going to do that because this happened or that happened." Perhaps they say, "If I go out there and I fail at this, then I'm never going to try it again." Or "I'm never going to do this again if I don't succeed the first time."

These are some of the most ridiculous comments I've ever heard. You are not going to win at everything the first time you do it. It isn't going to happen, and you can plan, plan, plan all day. If you do succeed at some things the very first try, that's great! Pat yourself on the back and keep moving to the next level.

Take a football team for example: They go out and play a strong, hard game and lose in the final seconds. They are devastated that they lost the game. Do you think that the team didn't prepare and plan to win? Of course they did. Everything that you plan doesn't always work according to your plan, but does this mean you should quit and never play another game?

There is something many people don't know about football. Every play that the offensive team uses is designed to score a touchdown. If it is designed to score, how come they don't score every single time? It is because the defense has other designs. Teams have to take into account that every play is not going to score, so they have to keep coming up with different strategies, different approaches, and different ways to do things.

Your plans and goals are the same: If you don't plan to win, yet have different strategies and approaches, you are setting yourself up for a long life of failure. You will never get yourself in the mindset of winning.

You must have the mindset of "Winning is not automatic; winning is not going to happen every time I go out; I'm going to do great."

Winning is about learning from your mistakes. That is the other side of this. You can't learn from a mistake if you don't make a mistake. You won't make a mistake unless you first take action, step out and try. But, you cannot sit back and wallow in your mistakes, either. You have to take action, and keep taking action over and over again.

A young lady I worked with had to pass an exam to get her license. She failed that test five times. Now, I know a lot of people would've quit or given in. Many people would've said, "This isn't for me, maybe I can't do this. Maybe I'm not strong enough; maybe I'm not smart enough. Maybe I don't know enough." This young woman, however, kept studying, kept striving, and kept fighting. She finally passed that test.

The question I have for you is, what would you do?

Would you fight, or would you quit? How big is your dream? How strong are your goals? Have you really set them in place so that you can succeed? Have you given yourself a plan B, a different way to approach things, or do you only have a plan A?

If you don't have a backup plan, what happens during an emergency? You don't quit; you come up with another plan. Do you take notice of your mistakes, your trials, and your tribulations, so that you can learn from them? If you don't do that, then you will always be held back. There will always be something or someone to hold you back in life, and it is usually you.

For instance, when planning marriage, people say, "We will get married once we get this in place, or once I take care of that." You have heard people say, "We are going to get married once we get enough money together." "We are going to get married once we move to this place, or once we get a house." Or, others say, "We are going to get married once the kids are born." There is always going to be something to hold you back.

Did you know that having wedding rings in order to get married is "tradition," but it is by no means required? If you are marrying for love, then you are marrying for the right reason. It seems silly to get married without rings, but if you don't have them and don't have the money to buy them, so what! If you really want to get married, just do it!

The same goes for business. "We are going to expand our business, once we get these things in position," or "We are going to buy that new office, once we get a certain amount of revenue coming in."

"Once we do this, we are going to get that." You've heard this before, in your personal growth, "I'm going to start losing weight once I get out of the bed, or find the right personal trainer." "I'm going to start this personal training program once I get the right foods that I want."

I had to have a coach tell me one time, "Stop making excuses and go to work." If you don't do that, the same thing will happen to you. You need to get a coach, but if you don't get off of your butt and do something, it doesn't matter who the coach is. You have to take action, and at some point say, "You know what, it's time for me to get off my ass and go to work."

Another thing we hold back on is actually moving forward in life. A lot of people want to start a business. Now, the first step in starting a business is finding out what your passion is. Why do you want to start a business? What goes into starting that particular business, and what does it take? Do you have the ability to start that type of business?

Not everyone who has a skill in a particular area has the ability to start a business. How long will it take you to get going, and are there are other requirements that you need to know about? Do you have an entrepreneurial spirit? Are you a natural leader, and can you delegate tasks gracefully?

You need to start taking action if you want to own your own business. The quicker you take action the better off you will be. If you don't do it now when you have the information, the knowledge, and the right kind of coach available to you, you will never know if your dreams will be fulfilled. There are a lot of people out there who miss out on their goals and dreams because they were waiting for everything to be perfect. Do you want to be one of them?

Do you know what the richest place in the world is? The graveyard. The graveyard is because there are millions of people there who have never fulfilled their dreams, because they didn't take action.

Do you want your dreams to be left in the grave while God is asking you why you didn't use your talents for His glory? The quicker you understand that you aren't perfect and neither is anyone else, the better.

There is one thing, and it may seem strange, but it's true nonetheless, that may help you understand if you have it in you to start a business: When you were a small child, did you ever have daydreams of piloting a plane or leading a safari? If you did fantasize about those types of things as a child, then more than likely, you have a natural inclination to start and run a business. It is similar, in a way, if you are up in front of a group of people, in control and loving every minute of it.

You love being the leader. But did you know that the Captain of a ship has full responsibility for everyone and everything on that ship? Likewise, you have that same responsibility as a business owner for the people working for you.

If you are going to be in control of other people's lives, jobs, and so forth, you must also be responsible, compassionate, and ready to move, even if everything isn't "perfect." Even if everyone isn't in their exact place at the moment, you have to trust that once you start moving that "ship" that they will eventually be in their place and do their job. Part of being a great leader is being graceful and merciful.

You must be somewhat stern as well, but it must be done in love. It is more like "tough love." If you are too mushy, sentimental, emotional, and forgiving, then you probably aren't cut out for business ownership. But if you have no problem telling your wife or husband that their breath really stinks, and they need to get to a dentist, then you probably have it in you to run a company.

Characteristics of a Perfectionist

1. **They Are Very Hard On Themselves–** Perfectionists are their
    own worst critics. They are also judgmental of others. I was a
    perfectionist as a musician, but I was also an achiever. I used to
    be with a band and between sets I would think about what we did
    wrong, so we could improve upon things for the next set.

2. **They Hate Mistakes-** Perfectionists don't believe something can
    go on well with mistakes in it. This belief is so not true. In my
    band, I was a vocalist, and we could've made many mistakes. I
    hated the mistakes, but the crowd still loved the music. I was great
    at covering up mistakes and turning our performances into some-
    thing better than they would've been without those mistakes. I
    didn't pay attention to the greatness in our band; I focused on our
    weaknesses instead.

3. **They Hate Not Being Seen As Perfect.** I hated to be seen as any-
    thing other than perfect; I used to tell my band mates not to make
    any mistakes. When I was on the stage I hated to look bad. If you
    didn't see me as perfect, no matter how much fun I could've had,
    I was always miserable in the end.

4. **They Are Very Defensive and Cannot Take Criticism Well, At
    All-** Sometimes you just have to just let things go. You cannot
    allow yourself to put up walls, even if you have been hurt in the
    past, because you didn't do something perfect, or were abused
    because of your perfectionism. If you are currently with a new set
    of people, a new family that would never dream of hurting you,
    then you are in the right place to begin your healing, and move
    forward with your future. It hurts a lot, and just like layers of an
    onion must be peeled, you must allow the layers of your heart to
    be peeled too. Open up and accept that criticism from someone
    that you know loves you. Even if you have to tell yourself 100
    times that you know that person loves you while looking in the
    mirror, then do it. "The wounds of a friend are intended to help,
    but an enemy's kisses are too much to bear" (GOD'S WORD
    Translation, Bible Gateway).

5. **They Are Never Satisfied, No Matter What The Outcome-** A
    perfectionist could be winning and everything can be going well,

but they still aren't satisfied. It is crazy; there is always something they think could've gone better. They will work and work and work to get something just the way they want it. The problem is, they think that their job is never done. A perfectionist may never see his dreams come to fruition, may never even cross the finish line.

6. **They Cannot Let Things Rest-** Let's say you have a project you have to work on. You've done your very best and it is ready. It cannot possibly be improved. The perfectionist will stay up all night and will still try to make it better until the very last second. Once the time is up, they will hand it in, and they still aren't satisfied with the outcome. That behavior is borderline psychotic, in my opinion.

7. **There Is No Middle Ground-** A perfectionist is either "Do or Die," "Feast or Famine." If they can't get something the way they want it, it must be shot to hell. Nothing else matters, they cannot see an alternative, and they close themselves off to any other way. They could be missing out on so many opportunities. When you open your mind to different ideas, there are so many possibilities. Stop trying to make it perfect "your way," because there are other methods to make things work.

8. **They Have To Win At Everything-** Perfectionists must be the best. Being "good" is not good enough; they have to be better than good. Being good kills them; it eats at them. It keeps them up at night. They cannot accept it. They pout, throw tantrums, hurt others emotionally and say harsh things to others because they cannot be the best. They can't admit that they aren't the best at everything and that they have faults, too. Perfectionists will try to fix everything, and if they cannot do it right, they will swear up and down that they can, and they will keep trying until it finally starts to work, even if it isn't.

9. **They Always Look At Life With The End In Mind-**This isn't always a bad trait, but you have to have an open mind, and realize that it isn't always going to end up the way it is in your mind, or in your goals and plans. Perfectionists do not realize that things aren't going to be that way all of the time, and they cannot accept that. If you are going to overcome perfectionistic tendencies, you need to accept that things aren't going to be the same as you originally intended.

Quotes About Perfectionism

"Perfection is not attainable, but if we chase perfection we can catch excellence." (Vince Lombardi)

"If you'll not settle for less than your best, you will be amazed at what you can accomplish in your lives." (Vince Lombardi)

"I think everyone should experience defeat at least once in their career. You learn a lot from it." (Lou Holtz)

"If you're not making mistakes, then you're not doing anything. I'm positive that a doer makes mistakes." (John Wooden)

"Excellence is the gradual result of always striving to do better." (Pat Riley)

"If you look for perfection you'll never be content." (Leo Tolstoy)

"Have no fear of perfection – you'll never reach it." (Salvador Dali)

"I am careful not to confuse excellence with perfection. Excellence, I can reach for; perfection is God's business." (Michael J. Fox)

"If people reach perfection they vanish, you know." (T.H. White)

"Nobody's perfect. We're all just one step up from the beasts and one step down from the angels." (Jeannette Walls)

"Too late, I found you can't wait to become perfect, you got to go out and fall down and get up with everybody else." (Ray Bradbury)

"Perfection is man's ultimate illusion. It simply doesn't exist in the universe...If you are a perfectionist; you are guaranteed to be a loser in whatever you do." (David Burns)

"The maxim, "Nothing prevails but perfection," may be spelled PARALYSIS." (Winston Churchill)

"Remember that fear always lurks behind perfectionism. Confronting your fears and allowing yourself the right to be human can, paradoxically, make you a far happier and more productive person." (David M. Burns)

"Stop waiting for the perfect day or the perfect moment...Take THIS day, THIS moment and lead it to perfection." (Steve Maraboli)

A Cautionary Tale –"R"

Ronnie was in love with Brenda. He wanted to propose to Brenda and get married. They had been dating for three years. Ronnie kept putting off the proposal, because he felt he wasn't making enough money to make Brenda happy. He also didn't have the perfect house or car that he wanted to share with Brenda, so he waited until everything was perfect.

Brenda just wanted to marry the man she loved.

He saw Brenda as being perfect, so Ronnie wanted everything to be perfect for her before he proposed. He kept trying to make himself into that perfect person.

After three years, Brenda got tired of waiting and met a man named Steve. Steve quickly came to realize that Brenda was a great woman.

He didn't have the things that Ronnie had; he wasn't even close. He wasn't striving for perfection. Gradually, he knew that he wanted to be with Brenda. He realized that Brenda wasn't looking for a perfect man and swept Brenda off of her feet, and Ronnie lost out.

The moral of the story is, you will never have everything perfect. Someone who is less than perfect will take your place if you don't let go of your perfectionistic tendencies. Then your original plan and dreams will be shot to hell. Don't be a Ronnie.

Chapter 6 –
You Gotta Believe

Faith, belief, and inspiration are the keys to abundant living. Faith gives you confidence that what you believe will eventually happen. Belief is what makes people do things, and it helps people make commitments. Inspiration gives you the motivation to keep going, even during the roughest of times. If you don't believe in something, you will fall for a lot of things, because you have nothing to stake your claim to or plant your feet in. You need to have something to believe in to keep you inspired.

Every beginning can provide a new and exhilarating challenge. Every dream provides hope and excitement. Anyone can do that. Anyone can have dreams, and some people even have a new dream every other day. The hard part is believing and working toward your goal. Sometimes, in order to keep persevering until the very end, you have to remind yourself why you had these dreams and goals to begin with. Completing a goal is much more difficult than thinking of one. Anything sounds interesting when it is brand new. However, if you don't have a real hearty interest in something, you won't make it to the end.

In order for you to keep going, there are two major things that you must consistently pay attention to. There are two areas of belief that you need to know about. One is self-belief. The lack of self-belief is the biggest thing that holds people back. They don't believe in themselves; but, there are a lot of things that can be done to change that. A lot of people don't believe they can do certain things. A lot of people have gone through life and enjoyed personal achievements. They may have had a lot of achievements; however, there is always one loss, or one major incident that may have stuck with them, giving them an unhealthy dose of self-doubt.

They say things like, "I can't do this," "I can't reach my goals" or "I can't achieve my dreams."

These thoughts creep into your mind and grow into weeds that destroy everything you have worked for. They can grow to overwhelming heights and manifest themselves into something very ugly. You must fight against the weeds in your mind and eventually kill them all. If you don't kill those weeds, you won't get past your first goal without tripping over them.

Unless you remove those weeds of doubt, you will continue to trip over them every time you have a new goal. It isn't always a lack of goals that will stop you either. You can have many great dreams and goals. You can even change your dreams and goals, because you think they are wrong, and you just don't seem able to move forward. What you really need to change is your own belief. Instead of doubting, believe in yourself, your goals, dreams, abilities, talents, and gifts. It may be hard work at first but don't give up. If you give up, you will eventually have another dream or goal at some point in the future, and the same thing will keep happening.

If you doubt yourself, it doesn't matter what other people believe about you, success won't happen for you. **You** have to believe that you can do things. This is one of the biggest things that hold people back. You can try to convince people to give up the self-doubt, but it can only be done by them and for them.

If they are trying to get attention, and trying to accomplish something to be noticed by a loved one, it won't be enough to keep them going, and it never will be. Only a belief in one's self, and not outside attention will sustain positive growth.

If, because of self-doubt, a person doesn't believe they can do anything, then they won't do anything. If we don't want to do something for ourselves, then we will never get it done. Accomplishments increase self-esteem, which in turn increases personal beliefs, which increases the desire to "do." This action will eventually bring about even more accomplishments.

If you don't have accomplishments, believe in what you want to accomplish. Believe in what you are capable of, and keep moving toward your goals.

There are a lot of people in certain situations who fold under pressure because they doubt themselves or their ability. They are afraid of what might happen afterwards if they try something.

Self-belief is a really big deal. In order to make it work for you, you must work on your "self." A lot of people don't know how to work on themselves. They continue to wallow in doubt and don't make any bold leaps of faith to do certain things. Let's take reading, for example. Reading books can improve you, and it is something that can get your self-belief going. If you tell yourself you can't do something, then you probably can't. If you tell yourself you can do something, then you probably can. It's really that simple. Your mind is like a computer. Whatever you program inside of your mind is what it will spit out.

If you keep saying that you aren't good at remembering names, then you have already convinced yourself that you cannot remember names. When you keep telling yourself that you cannot, you put the doubt in your mind that, "I can't do it." Self-doubt is what kills people. At one time in your past, you must have had a bad experience with memorizing names, and then felt really bad when you wanted to remember someone's name but you couldn't. You probably got so down on yourself you became crippled by self-pity. Am I right?

Self-pity brings depression, which also brings with it a feeling that you can't do anything, and you want others to feel sorry for you. Stop the victim mentality, and tell yourself that you can remember names. Tell yourself that you can do anything. If you tell yourself that you can remember names, and you start working at it, you won't be great at first, but you will eventually improve. This is the same for everything in life. But you have to have the belief in yourself that you can do it. If you don't believe in yourself, you are going to be in a world of trouble, so you have to change that. Remember: The lack of self-belief is the biggest crippler of a lot of people.

Another area of belief is belief in your goals, dreams and even in your business. One of the biggest things I deal with when I coach people in network marketing is recruiting. Those of you who are familiar with network marketing are already aware that recruiting is a big part of that business. A lot of people are afraid of recruiting. I have people tell me to my face that they don't want to recruit. This is weak thinking and will lead to business failure. It also shows a lack of self-belief. If someone truly believes in their business, why wouldn't they want to spread the word to others?

What is so paradoxical is the fact that they won't tell someone to their face about their marketing business, which is supposedly their passion, but they will tell you to your face with confidence, that they won't recruit. I tell people all of the time, there are only three reasons why people don't recruit:

1.   They don't know enough about their business
2.   They're lazy
3.   They don't believe in their business and/or what the company does

The last one permeates more than anything because most people just don't believe in what they are doing. If you believe in what you are doing, you will tell everyone. Let's say your organization had a cure for cancer. Are you going to tell me that you wouldn't go tell everyone that you can, especially those whom you know have cancer? Of course you would. You'd tell everybody. That is why you must make sure you have a business that you truly believe in.

If you can't believe in your business, then you aren't ready, yet. You must feel passionate about what you are doing. It is the same thing with your goals and your dreams. That is why I tell everybody, that you have to start writing things down, making a list. You have to start looking at this list every day. Whatever your goals and dreams are- start putting them on paper and start talking to people about them. Let people know what you are doing. Not what you are going to do "someday" but what you are doing right now. You are working at it now. But you have to believe that you are doing it. If you don't believe that you are doing it, it won't get done.

I'll give you another example: When I started working for a network marketing company in Maryland, I remember my first interview with my sponsor; I was asked, "What is it that you see yourself doing in the future?"

I told him I see myself moving to Atlanta in the near future.

After that, every time I talked to someone, my sponsor introduced me by saying, "Hi, this is Barrett, he is going to open up an office in Atlanta for us."

Do you see what was happening? I knew that it was something that I wanted to do, but I didn't fully believe it yet, because I hadn't done it. It took me three years to move to Atlanta.

But, what my sponsor did was sell me on my dream and my goal. Every time he introduced me to someone else, I heard my dream, making it more and more a part of my reality, and it wasn't so much of a dream anymore. I fully believed in it, moved to Atlanta, finally and opened up an office. I felt great and I was very proud of my accomplishment. I had said that's what I wanted to do, and that's what I did.

It's something that you have to set your mind to; if you don't, you are going to suffer from not believing in those dreams and goals. It will eat you up. If you don't believe in what you are doing, someone will come along with something else, and you will get caught up in that and you will never get back to what you were doing. So many people are sitting at a desk today that belongs to someone else, because they didn't have enough faith in themselves, or their dreams to pursue them. They are corporate grumps, they might be in management, but they are not happy. They aren't happy because they aren't doing what they really want to do, and they are caught up in the "Rut of Life."

I'm a believer that people can talk about their goals and dreams all they want to, but until they start to work on them, they don't fully believe. You can't tell me that they fully believe if they haven't taken action. I'm a firm believer that actions speak louder than words. Many people say they believe, but their actions say differently. Actions will tell you the truth.

One thing people hear me say all the time is that I don't like the word "try." People sometimes say, "Nothing beats a failure but a try." I don't like that phrase. The reason is because when people say they are going to try something, I don't believe them.

Picture yourself in a car and your car breaks down on the side of the road. You get on your cell phone and you call your best friend, and you tell them you need them to come and pick you up.

Your best friend says, "I'm going to try to get there."

How much belief do you have in that statement? Do you really believe that they are going to be there? Or would you think that you need to call someone else?

"Try" is a word that people use to appease someone who expects something from them.

Many people say, "I'll try to do it, I'll try to be there, I'll try to show up, and I'll try to get this done," instead of saying, "I'm going to do it. I will be there."

If you are stranded on the side of the road, wouldn't you want your friend to say, "I'll be there," or "I can't make it," so that way you will know for sure if you need to call someone else? Belief is something that is always shown. Actions are what show that belief. You have to have belief in what you do.

You have probably heard the saying by Henry Ford. He says, "The person who believes they can, and the person who believes they can't, are both usually right."

So, you have to decide if you are going to be someone who believes in what you do. Or are you going to let someone else dictate your life?

Quotes About Belief

"In order to succeed, we must first believe that we can." (Michael Korda)

"It is not important what you believe, only that you believe." (Unknown Author)

"The fact of the matter is that there is no hip world, there is no straight world. There is a world, you see, which has people in it who believe in a variety of different things. Everybody believes in something and everybody, by virtue of the fact that they believe in something, uses that something to support their own existence." (Frank Zappa)

"Believe in yourself. Have faith in your abilities. Without a humble but reasonable confidence in your own powers, you cannot be successful or happy. (Norman Vincent Peale)

"Nobody can make you feel inferior without your consent." (Eleanor Roosevelt)

"It's not who you are that holds you back, it's who you think you're not." (Anonymous Source)

"The thing always happens that you really believe in, and the belief in things makes it happen." (Frank Lloyd Wright)

"Live your beliefs and you can turn the world around." (Henry David Thoreau)

"Your belief determines your action, and your action determines your results. But first, you have to believe." (Unknown Author)

"Big dreams create the magic that stirs men's souls to greatness." (Vince Lombardi)

"Faith is about doing. You are how you act, not just how you believe." (Mitch Albom)

"Follow your bliss and the universe will open doors for you where there were only walls." (Joseph Campbell)

"To accomplish great things we must not only act, but also dream; not only plan, but also believe." (Anatole France)

"For those who believe, no proof is necessary. For those who don't believe, no proof is possible." (Stuart Chase)

"Sometimes we fight who we are, struggling against ourselves and our natures. But we must learn to accept who we are and appreciate who we become. We must love ourselves for what and who we are, and believe in our talents." (Harley King)

"Don't be afraid of the space between your dreams and reality. If you can dream it, you can make it so." (Belva Davis)

"Belief creates behaviors." (Neale Donald Walsch)

"Always remember to take your Vitamins: Take your Vitamin A for ACTION, Vitamin B for BELIEF, Vitamin C for CONFIDENCE, Vitamin D for DISCIPLINE, Vitamin E for ENTHUSIASM!!" (Pablo)

"Belief, hard work, love – you have those things, you can do anything." (Mitch Albom)

"To quote Gandhi yet again, "If I have the belief that I can do it, I shall surely acquire the capacity to do it even if I may not have it at the beginning." (Jeff Yeager)

"Belief isn't simply a thing for fair times and bright days I think. What is belief – what is faith – if you don't continue in it after failure?" (Brandon Sanderson)

"To believe and yet to have no hope is to thirst beside a fountain." (Ann-Marie MacDonald)

A Cautionary Tale–"E"

Evelyn decided she wanted to join a network marketing business. She recruited Stanley, John, and Mary. Stanley and John ended up quitting. That left her with Mary, who recruited Tonya. Tonya went on to recruit Bob, who started doing great things. Then, Mary decided to quit, because she didn't see what it was doing for her, and she didn't believe in the business.

Oddly enough, Evelyn ended up quitting, as well, because she didn't see things happening the way she wanted. She didn't believe in what she was doing, and didn't believe in herself either. After all this, Bob rolled up to Evelyn's sponsor, whose name was Michael. Michael said, "Let's keep this train rolling."

Bob became the top producer in the entire company. Why? Because Bob believed that he could, he believed in the company, and believed what could eventually happen for him.

Unfortunately, all the others fell by the wayside because they didn't believe. They went back to jobs that they didn't like, and went back to dealing with the "rut" of life, forever.

Because they didn't believe, they never accomplished their dreams and goals in life.

Please, don't be an Evelyn.

Chapter 7 –
Getting Things in Order

Getting things in order is about priorities. The one thing that people don't know how to do is put things in their proper order so as to reach optimum success. The author, Steven Covey wrote, "Most of us spend too much time on what is urgent, and not enough time on what is important."

We make things urgent sometimes when they aren't urgent but are just important. We don't address the real urgency in our lives. We actually put things out of order and in doing so, we miss out on things that could've gotten done, because we put too much priority on them, and not enough priority on the other things.

Sometimes we purposely put our dreams on the back burner to give way to things that shouldn't be a priority. Let me give you an example: If your dreams are to someday open up a restaurant, but you focus on playing in a softball league instead, or you focus on doing things with your kids instead. Your kids are important, but if you talk to them about your dream, they will also understand that their parents want to open up a restaurant.

A lot of the time we keep our dreams inside, and we end up working on other things, and we never ever "get there." Sometimes, we focus on things we cannot change, when we should focus on the things we can change, or at least what can bring about the desired change.

Talking to someone about your dreams and goals, as long as you are truly serious, is the best way to start. If you're not serious, don't waste your time or theirs. Make sure you have your ideas written down, as well.

Now, this is a touchy subject with a lot of people because, many people cannot handle what I am about to say. Let's take for instance if you have a death in the family. This happened to me, and I was very close to this person, and I loved them with all of my heart.

At the viewing, I was the first one there, the very first one there. I was also one of the first people to leave. I left because I had a business meeting that I needed to get to. I caught some flak from some family members about leaving early, but here's what people don't understand; I had to ask myself this question, "Can I change the situation; can I bring this person back?"

"Is my not being there going to hurt that particular person?"

No. Unfortunately, they were gone, and I could not hurt them by leaving the viewing. Then, since the funeral was the very next day, I asked myself another question. "Was I going to be at the funeral?"

Yes, I was going to be there all day with my family.

With that answer, I didn't feel that guilty about leaving early. I knew I had been there when this person was alive-they were a part of me; that was the most important part-that I had my memories, and that carried me on, and I was there for them after they had passed when it was necessary.

Now, when it came to prioritizing my day and going to my meeting, there was one thing a lot of people didn't take into consideration and that was my relationship with the deceased. This relative was one of the most supportive people of my business. They were the type of person that would come to me and say, "What are you doing home; you should be working on your business."

They would also say, "I know you are going to do great, I know you are going to be a success, and I believe in you." They always told me these things.

When it came down to me being at the viewing of the body, or going to that meeting, the decision was made, and it made me feel good to know that I was doing what they would have me do. I put my priorities in order to know what was important; to live my life the way they would want me to live.

That is one of the things a lot of us don't do, because we think in terms of, "Am I being selfish by going?" Well, if the person is supportive of me doing my business; it wasn't selfish, because I was doing what they would want me to do, anyway.

Here's what we always think: "What are other people going to think?"

Those other people don't really have much to do with anything. They don't amount to a hill of beans when it comes to the real scheme of things. So, you have to ask yourself, "Am I doing this for me, or am I doing this for 'other people'?" Because the other people are those who will say, "I didn't think you were going to do anything, anyway," if your business fails or your dreams don't come to fruition.

So, you need to fight through that, and put things in priority and in the right order. Focus on the things that will bring about change or bring about the desired change. You don't know if it is going to be the thing that will make it happen for you, but at least put yourself in a position that later on could make it happen.

When it comes to talking about priorities, you have to think about what comes first in life. We have a lot of things in our daily activity that we need to do. How many of you take the time to write down the daily activities or tasks that you need to do? I'm not talking about your schedule; I'm talking about the tasks that you need to take care of in order to make the day run more smoothly.

Well, a lot of times we don't get them done, because we don't write them down. I'm suggesting that you write everything down so that you can look at the tasks throughout the day; that way you don't forget to get them done. You can write them in your planner, put them in your cell phone, record them in your cell phone and play them back, use a voice recorder and play that back. I write them on my sticky pad.

I say to myself, there are seven things every day, that I need to accomplish. I just write down what those seven things are. They change every day for me. Some things can stay consistent for you. If you know that every day you need to work-out, put that on there. If you know that you need to pray every day, put that on there. If there are things that you want to put in place to make sure that you are living your life the way you want to, put that on there, and then cross them off when you have done them. It brings a great sense of pride to have put things in some type of order for your day, write everything down, and then look at your list of crossed off accomplishments.

Now comes the hard part: which comes first? Which 'task' is more important than the others? What is something I must get done that if I don't, my life is going to become worse? You need to make sure that you put things in the right order; that is where prioritization comes in. You need to separate the things that are important from those that are urgent. "If I don't get it done today, will it hurt me?"

"If I get it done today or if I don't, will my life be O.K.?" You need to ask yourself those questions.

You heard me mention Steven Covey, earlier. Steven Covey is a great author, and he authored a book called, "The Seven Habits of Highly Effective People." He also wrote another book called, "First Things First." In that book he talks about priorities. He talks about the four quadrants in his time management matrix. The matrix outlines about what's important and what's urgent; what needs to be moved from important to urgent, and what needs to be moved from urgent to important. We do a lot of things in life that are important to us, and that are urgent to us. Urgency carries a different weight with it. It gives the idea that, *'You have to get it done right now, and if you don't get it done right now there is going to be a negative consequence, or someone is going to pay for it somewhere along the line.'*

Important means that it is something that cannot go without being done, because it has weight, as well, but it doesn't have to be done right away. I will give you an example: In one quadrant, you have a sick friend in the hospital; in another you have to go do business and close a sale so that you can collect a check; in another someone tells you about a television show you just must see, and in another you may have an errand that you have to get done. In the end, you have to ask yourself which is the most important, or the most urgent.

Many of you will say that going to see your sick friend is the most urgent, or you may say that you need to see that television show because it won't be on again. Some of you may think that you have to run that errand because you need to get that done so that you can finish everything else. Or, you may think, it's best to close that sale and get the check to pay the bills.

Which one is a priority to you, I cannot say. You have to decide which one is a priority for you, and which area you have to focus on first, because it will help you determine how to proceed with the rest of your tasks. If you don't put them in some type of order, you will end up running around willy-nilly like a chicken with its head cut off, and you won't remember what's important and what's urgent, and then even more things will pile up.

If you don't have a system to put everything in order, your daily life will be a mess; you will be stressed and maybe even miss deadlines. Do you have any idea how missing deadlines can mess up everything else? It is like a domino effect. Eventually, you will be so stressed out over missing so many things, that you end up giving up completely. If you want to fulfill your dreams and goals, everything else that isn't as important, must be put on the back burner. Don't miss an opportunity to fulfill your dreams.

Being responsible and faithful is important, not only in business, but also in your everyday life. People won't continue to trust in you, and you may even lose out on a job or a business opportunity if you are not responsible. Even if you are more talented, the next person, who can be counted on, and who deserves just as much of a chance as you do, will get that new assignment, and you will be stuck in the mud.

If you feel like you have a problem with time management, make a schedule. Go to bed early, cut out some television shows, wake up a little earlier, and don't rush through life.

If your friends want to go out, you may have to say no if you have deadlines. Or, you can make sure that you finish everything that is urgent; then finish everything that is important, and then allow yourself some relaxation. If that means you have to take a rain check on going out with your friends for an entire month, then don't be afraid to say, "I can't go out for a while because I have too much to catch up on." You will feel much better knowing that your list is crossed off, and when you do finally go out, you won't have that stress to carry around with you.

Quotes About Priorities (Getting Things in Order)

"The mark of a great man is one who knows when to set aside the important things in order to accomplish the vital ones." (Brandon Sanderson)

"Perpetual devotion to what a man calls his business is only to be sustained by perpetual neglect of other things." (Robert Louis Stevenson)

"Good for you, and be proud of yourself because you have your priorities in order. Be proud of yourself if you are responsible, reliable, and persistent, and take your job and education seriously." (Ann Monarch)

"You will need to make time for your family no matter what happens in your life." (Matthew Quick)

"Action expresses priorities." (Mahatma Gandhi)

"A simple life is not seeing how little we can get by with – that's poverty – but how efficiently we can put first things first....When you're clear about your purpose and your priorities, you can painlessly discard whatever else does not support these, whether it's clutter in your cabinets or commitments on your calendar." (Victoria Moran)

"The most important thing in life is knowing the most important things in life." (David F. Jakielo)

"Persistence. Perfection. Patience. Power. Prioritize your passion. It keeps you sane." (Criss Jami)

"We do not have a money problem in America. We have a values and priorities problem." (Marian Wright Edelman)

"Good things happen when you get your priorities straight." (Scott Caan)

"The key is not to prioritize what's on your schedule, but to schedule your priorities." (Steven Covey)

"Decide what you want, decide what you are willing to exchange for it. Establish your priorities and go to work." (H.L. Hunt)

"In all planning you make a list and you set priorities." (Alan Lakein)

A Cautionary Tale – "E"

Edward is one of ten children. His mother was in the hospital, and he berated his siblings because they went to work while their mom was in the hospital all day. They came to visit Mom after they got off work, but he was mad because he spent all day in the hospital with her. She was all drugged up, sick and asleep most of the day, so he stayed in the lobby for the majority of the time drinking coffee, and eating hospital food, bored and worried.

Edward's siblings came to visit later in the evening, but they did come every day. He gave them the blues, because he wanted them there all day. His siblings told him, "Edward, all we can do is pray for Mom, and hope that she gets better because none of us are doctors." That wasn't good enough for Edward. He spent all day worrying at the hospital for his Mom.

When Mom finally got better, the siblings got together- they had to pay the hospital bill. Since Edward spent all those days with Mom and hadn't been working, he had no money to contribute.

When Mom got much better, the siblings got together and sent their Mom on a cruise. They wanted her to have a special time after being so sick for so long, and because they wanted her to know, "We love you, we took care of you, and we are here for you."

When Mom got better, she was so thankful for her children who paid her bill and sent her on the trip; she thanked them profusely, but not Edward.

Edward hadn't contributed to what she knew. She didn't know that Edward had been there all day, every day, while she was in the hospital. Why? Because she had been so sick, asleep and on drugs, and she didn't know that anyone was there.

Edward felt really awful that he couldn't contribute to her trip; he also felt bad for not taking care of priorities and working. The moral of this story is that you have to put things in order. You have to discern, what's important, what's urgent, and at the end of the day, how will it turn out for you?

Don't be like Edward. Make sure that you are putting things in order, because you know at the end of every day you have to be accountable for something.

Chapter 8 –
Lazy Days

There are so many people out there who are lazy, let's face it. Not everybody wants to work. Actually, there are very few people who work; they say it's the 20/80 rule, where 20% of the people do 80% of the work. The rest are lazy; they just don't want to get up, get out, and get it done.

If you are one of the 20% you might attribute it to a number of things, but, if you know what you need to do, and just don't do it, you will spiral into a downward hole of apathy. It can be considered spiritual apathy, lethargy, slothfulness, or just straight-up laziness. Many things will come up in life to make you not want to work.

Slothfulness is one of the seven deadly sins, and I think it is apparent as to why. If you work, then you will keep working. If you stop, even for a short period of time, except for vacations, you will get to a point where you just don't want to do anything. You get lazy or slothful, and that's why it is deadly. Everything just stops. You have come to "the end" of yourself at this point. Even your lack of money, negative bank account, or debts piling up won't get you moving, again.

Most people don't even know that they are lazy, and even if they know it, they won't admit it. Slothfulness comes with a bad connotation and most people don't want to be called lazy. Deep inside they really don't want to give in to their laziness. So, when someone calls you lazy, the first thing you do is defend yourself saying, "I'm not lazy," and maybe you will even bring up an example of something you have done to try and prove that you aren't lazy. That doesn't mean you aren't lazy or won't be seen as lazy.

Perception is so vital. If people see you as lazy, they don't want to deal with you. No one wants to deal with a lazy person. Would you? If you don't have drive, if you don't have initiative, if you don't have that get-up-and-go attitude, then people won't deal with you. So, if you are seen as lazy, then you need to make some changes.

I remember a job I had as a teenager, and the other guys thought I was lazy. As a matter of fact, they nicknamed me "sleepy," because I had to be at work, and was always sleepy at 5:30 in the morning. As a teenager I didn't want to get up that early. There were certain times when I could admit I was lazy, when I was called to do the work, I did it. But it is all a matter of perception. They perceived me as being lazy, even though I really wasn't; I did the work I had to do, and when I didn't have work to do, I would fall asleep. That is what they saw.

It is all about how others see you.

You can work hard but have a slothful attitude. If you sound miserable while you are working, then you probably aren't happy with your job. If you aren't happy, then you aren't going to work as hard as you would if you were excited about what you did for a living. It is a choice that you make. You can be a cashier and be excited about your job if you choose to do so. That will automatically cause you to work harder, and then others will not see you as lazy.

Even if you take more breaks than the average person, if you have a good attitude and work hard during your shifts, people either won't notice that you are taking extra breaks. Or, they will believe you deserve to have that extra time because you worked so hard.

There's one other possibility: If you work very hard and have a great work attitude, people will begin to trust you more. Instinctively they will assume, if they don't see you, that you are working, but that you are just somewhere else, helping someone. This is why perception is not limited to what you can "see" with your eyes; sometimes it is about what you know to be true because of their attitude.

Here's the cold hard truth: Laziness is real, it is genuine. Many people just don't want to work. Laziness is not something that people want to wear as a "badge of honor," so they avoid being called that. Here's another thing people avoid: Work.

Since the dawn of Man, ever since man had the opportunity to put something off, Man has put it off. When Man had to start thinking, "What lies ahead of me, what's in the future, what's coming up?" Man would start rationalizing, "Is that something I need to do right now, or can I sleep on it and do it in the morning, or even do it next week?" That is when Man started developing laziness.

We are all given free will and free choice. Yet, sometimes what we choose or "will" to do, or rather "not to do" are to our detriment. We need to focus on things that will put us in a positive position, and usually that means work.

This is why God has always told us that work is for our own good, and that we have to work if we wanted food. The Bible says, "If you don't work, you don't eat." (2 Thessalonians 3) We were created to work by the "sweat of our brow" through planting seeds, tilling fields, and taking care of crops. However, not everyone farms anymore. There are so many different types of work to do, but no matter what, we need to do **something**. Even volunteering is working.

A wise lady, who taught me some of the things I know, named Peggy Hightower, asked me a question, "Which came first, did God give Adam work first, before the fall of Eden, or did God give man work after the fall of Eden?"

I've heard people answer, "God gave Adam work as punishment." That's not true. God gave Adam work at the very beginning, even before He gave him Eve. Adam's blessing was to "work" the Garden of Eden. So, when you look at things in retrospect, work is actually a blessing.

Ironic, then, that we spend our entire lives running from the blessing we were given. Think about how our lives would be different if we ran to that blessing and embraced work for what it is. How much better off would we be? Laziness costs so much in life, because we blow things off, we procrastinate, and we lose out on so many things because of laziness.

It seems like laziness becomes a habit that just sticks to you. You now have to work even harder to get unstuck. Instead of trying to get unstuck, you can stop laziness right in its tracks. It is going to take some will power, but if you catch it and get to it before it gets to you, then you will not have to work to peel that glue off. You just have to work- period.

Here's an example: I'm a member of B.N.I., which stands for Business Networking International. When I was looking for a chapter to join I tested out a few different meetings first.

I was first introduced to B.N.I. by a gentleman who ran a home inventory business. He took me to a meeting that was far away, over an hour from my home, and they met early in the morning. When I went, I saw a lot of business people networking, and a lot of potential.

I said, "Wow, this is something really cool, but is there anything closer to home because this is a heck of a drive, especially during rush hour traffic in the morning." He told me that they have several chapters, and he was certain that there was one nearer my home.

I decided to look online to find a location near me. In my search, I found one, and went to the meeting; again they met in the morning. They even offered breakfast, but I didn't feel comfortable there. There were many great business people there; they were very nice, and I enjoyed myself. Nonetheless, I just didn't feel right being there. Typically, at a meeting like this, I want to give referrals, as well as, receive them, and I just didn't feel that there was a good fit there.

So, I decided to visit another group. They also met in the mornings, and I immediately felt comfortable because I saw a gentleman there with whom I had gone to school. That made me feel good. Familiarity makes anyone feel more comfortable.

Before I joined, however, I wanted to visit one more group, just to make sure. So I visited one that was very close to me. This particular group happened to meet at noon.

Now, you have to understand that I am not a person who likes to get up early in the morning. I like to get up when God wakes me up. I don't even feel obligated to wake up before the sun comes up, so you can tell that I liked this group a whole lot better because I didn't have to wake up early in the morning to get there.

So, I went and visited, but I didn't feel comfortable at all. I felt that some of the members behaved unprofessionally and this wasn't the type of group I wanted to deal with.

I came to the conclusion, after visiting both morning and afternoon groups, that the morning group was a better fit for me. I thought- you know what, the people that really want to go to work, the people that want to get things done, and those that take their business more seriously are willing to get up and go to work. They don't mind getting out of bed, even if it is uncomfortable.

If you work with someone who is lazy, they probably aren't very successful.

They may even say things like, "I'm so tired today, I wish it was Friday, already," or "I wish I was at home in bed right now." If you have a job and on Monday you are already wishing that it was Friday, then you aren't happy with what you do. You are just existing and floating through life. You don't know what real abundant living is. It is as if you are a zombie. Do you want to be a zombie forever? Do you want to spend your life always looking at the clock? I'd rather have a job every day where I never look at the clock because I have so much to do, and I also love doing it. I want to work without having to remember what day of the week it is. This happens more often for people who work from home, work for themselves, and work hard.

Success and comfort don't mix. Lazy people are usually self-centered and want everything handed to them on a silver platter. If you haven't conquered laziness yet, then you aren't ready to work from home. You must be disciplined first. Even if it means you have to work for a certain period of time in order to get something done, then you have to do so, and not take a break. It is better to work 10 hours straight with no breaks, than to work a few hours and get nothing done, and then feel bad. If you have to work three days in a row, then do it, and take a two day break if you can. Or, rather, if you have to work 10 or 12 days in a row without a day of rest, then do it, as long as you intend to refresh yourself for two days and not just one.

If you aren't disciplined enough to get out of bed in the morning because you were up late watching "Family Guy," then you won't be disciplined enough to not watch it, so that you can go to bed early (I don't understand how anyone can stay in bed so long, anyway. It starts getting uncomfortable and you begin regretting not going to work because now you are missing out on earning money). You will never be successful as long as you are making yourself comfy and cozy lying in bed all day, or sitting on the couch with the remote, drinking beer all day. You are going to have to step out of your "comfort" zone; get out of the "lazy man" zone, and into the "hard work" zone.

I was successful because I stepped out of my comfort zone. I joined the morning B.N.I. chapter, and I have been a member for years. I enjoy the experience, and I get several referrals from business owners. People take me seriously, now. Why do you think that is? Because I got up and stepped out of my comfort zone and made it happen for me.

You don't just stumble out of bed one day and find a million dollars lying on the floor. You get out of bed, you work, you invest, you work some more, you make contacts, you work some more, and then you do it all over again the next day. You move forward with your goals and dreams, and eventually one day, you just might be a millionaire. For some it may be very slow progress, and for others it may be fast. Either way, God knows what is best for you.

If He knows you don't know how to manage your time, then He knows you definitely won't be able to manage your money correctly. It is called stewardship, and you have to be able to handle your life before you can start a business. If you have to save money by avoiding Starbucks every day to show God that you are serious about your future, then do it. That is $5 a day, which is $35 a week, which turns out to be $140 a month. When it adds up, it becomes a lot. If there are other things that you are blowing money on, then you need to ask yourself if those things are truly necessary. You will find that most are not, so stop. Every little thing adds up.

This all comes back down to laziness, because you could make coffee at home and buy the extras that you like. That would save you plenty of money. There are always ways around things.

Do you wonder if you are lazy, yet do not see yourself as being lazy at all? Ask yourself some questions and see if any of these statements remind you of yourself: If you have ever said, "I'm going to go work out today, but…" and thrown in "after I do this" or "after I take a nap" or "I'll start next week once I get things in order," then you may be lazy.

If you ever said upon waking up in the morning, "I'm going to get up and cook dinner in a little while," and after a half hour goes by, you say, "I'll just order out again, because I don't feel like cooking right now." then you may be a little lazy.

Or if you are self-employed and you say, "I think I'm going to go to work today or maybe not." Or "I may do something today, or maybe I won't," then you might be a little lazy.

Even if you work for someone else, you may be lazy. That may be a shocker, but many people choose a job where they sit behind a desk all day, and don't have to answer to anyone. As long as they do their little bit of tasks, they still get a paycheck, even though they are sitting on their behind all day long. Unfortunately, that is laziness too, because they aren't trying to achieve anything more in life.

If we work hard during the day, we will have sweet sleep at night. Many people can't sleep at night because they don't do enough during the day. Then they complain to their family and even to their doctors, saying, "I need something to help me sleep at night, I have trouble falling asleep." Granted there are some people who work hard and still have insomnia. This could be due to a lack of physical movement and/or exercise. You are probably doing a lot. However, when you don't get physical movement, while you sit in an office, your brain is working and at the end of the day, it needs rest. However, your body is still at rest and doesn't need a "break," per se. You need to ask yourself, if you are someone who is willing to step out of your comfort zone.

Another example of someone being lazy is taking the time to pick up this book. You may have read Chapter 8, and said to yourself, "I'm going to read Chapter 9, tomorrow." Then tomorrow comes, and you say, "Maybe I'll read it next week or next month." That comes back to laziness, too, because you have good intentions, but you don't have good follow-through. So, actually, you don't have any actions at all.

Laziness costs you a lot in life, but I think you already know that because that is why you are reading this book. It can cost you opportunities. How many times have you been someplace, and someone told you that you just missed something. I bet, if you retraced your steps, some of what held you up can be traced back to just being lazy. Some of it can go back to you saying, "I'll sleep an extra 10 or 15 minutes this morning, and **then** I'll get up and go." By the time you got there you missed something.

Laziness can also lead to bad habits. Lazy people neglect things, themselves, and other people. They start to get different habits that cause others to have a negative perception of them. So, you want to make sure that you stay away from laziness.

Laziness can also cost you the people working with you. A lot of people will shy away from you, and run from you if they know you are lazy. If that perception is given about you, watch, people will stay away from you. Who wants to work with someone who is lazy?

It will also cost you your own sanity. You will continue to put off so many things in your life, and it will cost you in the long run. For example, if you continue to put off exercise, eventually you will end up on the operating table, and have open heart surgery, right after you have a heart attack. It can cost you your ambition. Sometimes you can sit around on your couch not wanting to do anything.

The next thing you know, "lazy" is who you are. You become that person who never wants to accomplish anything. You will start giving excuses for everything and anything. That is what it looks like when you lose your ambition, and you will be the only one who doesn't notice it. Everyone else around you will notice it, and they will get tired just looking at you.

So, how do you overcome laziness? That is what people often ask. It is something that you can change. One way is to do one thing at a time. You don't need to do everything all at once, because you can't possibly do everything at once, anyway. Focus on doing only one thing at a time. You can also break projects down into smaller pieces so that you can handle them, and make it a little easier. You also need to see the end result. You have to make sure you know what your end goal is and that you can see it, then you can go get it. Someone once told me, "If you can 'sees' it, then you can 'seize' it."

Think about what might happen in the end, if you don't accomplish your tasks and goals. I knew a lady once who was basically raising her children to be lazy. Her children were very disrespectful; they didn't want to do anything, and she didn't want to discipline them because she was lazy. She was turning them into people who were disrespectful, irresponsible, and lazy. She never gave them any disciplinary action and never whopped their behinds; they never had any consequences for their actions, or lack thereof. You can really hurt children by not disciplining them.

What are the benefits of not being lazy? Are you going to receive a reward of some type, such as any of the following?

- Are you going to reach your goal?
- Are you going to get praise?
- Are you going to get recognition?

What is your goal? By doing something, and not being lazy, will that help you achieve it? One thing you need to do in order to stop being lazy is to get your rest. You also need to get exercise and put your body in use in a natural form. Once your body is flowing with that positive energy of rest and exercise, you will have a stable feeling of well-being, and you will be able to get a lot more accomplished.

Another thing is that you need to be inspired. You need to find something that drives you from inside that is bigger than your vision. Something that makes you feel you can accomplish anything as long as you keep focused on whatever that inspiration is. As long as you focus on that inspiration and let it guide you, you will do great, and then laziness won't even exist anymore.

Quotes on Laziness

"The Pain of Discipline or the Pain of Regret. Take your pick." (Unknown)

"We often miss opportunity because it's dressed in overalls and looks like work." (Thomas A. Edison)

"Procrastination is my sin. It brings me naught but sorrow. I know that I should stop it. In fact, I will – tomorrow." (Gloria Pitzer)

"If your dream is a big dream, and if you want your life to work on the high level that you say you do, there's no way around doing the work it takes to get you there." (Joyce Chapman)

"Sloth makes all things difficult, but industry all easy; and he that riseth late must trot all day, and shall scarce overtake his business at night; while laziness travels so slowly, that poverty soon overtakes him." (Benjamin Franklin)

"Habitual procrastinators will readily testify to all the lost opportunities, missed deadlines, failed relationships and even monetary losses incurred just because of one nasty habit of putting things off until it is often too late." (Stephen Richards)

"Knowledge without application is like a book that is never read." (Christopher Crawford, Hemel Hempstead)

"Laziness may appear attractive, but work gives satisfaction." (Anne Frank)

"So much attention is paid to the aggressive sins, such as violence and cruelty and greed with all their tragic effects that too little attention is paid to the passive sins, such as apathy and laziness, which in the long run can have a more devastating effect." (Eleanor Roosevelt)

"The idle man does not know what it is to enjoy rest." (Albert Einstein)

"Sloth and silence are a Fool's Virtues." (Benjamin Franklin)

"The present generation, wearied by its chimerical efforts, relapses into complete indolence. Its condition is that of a man who has only fallen asleep towards morning: first of all come great dreams, then a feeling of laziness, and finally a witty or clever excuse for remaining in bed." (Soren Kierkegaard)

"Know the true value of time; snatch, seize, and enjoy every moment of it. No idleness, no laziness, no procrastination; never put off till tomorrow what you can do today." (Lord Chesterfield)

"Aim at perfection in everything, though in most things it is unattainable. However, they who aim at it, and persevere, will come much nearer to it than those whose laziness and despondency make them give it up as unattainable." (Lord Chesterfield)

"Failure is not our only punishment for laziness; there is also the success of others." (Jules Renard)

"Laziness never arrived at the attainment of a good wish." (Miguel de Cervantes)

"Laziness is a secret ingredient that goes into failure. But it's only kept a secret from the person who fails." (Robert Half)

"A year from now you may wish you had started today." (Karen Lamb)

A Cautionary Tale –"X"

Xena, a young girl in graduate school, had to take care of her two year old daughter. She worked from home, but she wanted to step it up a bit and start a company. Xena wanted to start creating websites with her husband, Ben, since he was a graphic designer and she was a writer. Their goal was to eventually sell these websites, so they could create a better life for their daughter.

However, Xena had a weakness. She felt loneliness during the day. When her husband was home at night, she wanted to spend a little time with him. Instead of spending time with him in starting up this new company, she wanted to watch movies with him every night. Xena could've easily allowed time for both of them on the weekend. She was being lazy, and their time spent together making websites would have been just as special, if not, more so. If Xena would've spent time with her husband working on the websites instead of watching television, things would have been so much different. She realized that and began to do that.

They were making progress, but because of stress, Xena went back to her old ways. Her husband wasn't disciplined enough to keep going without her so went along with everything that she wanted. Soon enough, she became pregnant again. This was a very difficult pregnancy for Xena. She needed so much help from Ben and her best friend that they just couldn't work on any websites together. They were able to make a decent living, but they never had the ability to go on a nice vacation together.

They could've spent time together traveling the country, or the world for that matter, if Xena wouldn't have been lazy.

Her dreams were never fulfilled, and now she is a full time mom working from home. Laziness can be overcome when it is absolutely necessary. When trying to fulfill one's dreams however, laziness is an easy escape. Don't be a Xena

Chapter 9 –
Stronger than Pride

Pride is one of the biggest things that holds us back. The title of this book is called, "Why Didn't You Get It Done?" and one of the reasons we don't get it done is because we are too proud. We don't accept help; we don't ask for help, and we try to do everything by ourselves. I have something to tell you: We were not put on this earth to be independent. We were put here to be interdependent. This means we have to depend on each other to get things done.

You may not like this idea, but even the God who created us this way wasn't and isn't alone in Heaven, and I'm not just talking about angels, either. God has the number one spot, of course, but God is a "trinity," which includes a relationship with His son Jesus, and the Holy Spirit. God was giving us an example that we need one another and cannot make it alone, if even He didn't try to go it alone.

Now, I understand that it is hard to trust people at times, but we must give them the benefit of the doubt. Opening yourself up in sharing your dreams and goals with others isn't easy, but you have to let people in, in order to get where you want to be.

What if your best friend is in your life for a reason? What if God, Himself, put that person in your life because He knew that you two would be a perfect match to go into business together? Maybe you are being tested in order to see if you are willing to depend on another person for help and to be more humble.

Humility is the opposite of pride, but we have such a hard time being humble. Sometimes you have to show people a vulnerable side, or let people help you because it is good for you and for them to help. Pride's definition is a sense of happiness or accomplishment. You can be proud of your child scoring a touchdown in a game, or getting all A's. We can be proud of ourselves for getting a promotion. Those are great accomplishments that we should be very proud of. But there is also a pride that holds you back. We don't allow ourselves to get to that next level because we are still holding on to the one thing that keeps us from letting someone else in. We won't allow another person to be a part of our lives, or allow them to help us. We have too much pride and feel that we have to do things alone, and with that, we ruin our ambition. We ruin things that could have come our way.

Don't let pride hold you back, because it can, and it will. Not only will pride hold you back, but it will knock you down, punch your lights out, and kick you in the face, as well. Pride is a deadly force not to be reckoned with.

Some people are very ambitious, driven, and always strive to do their best. But I guarantee you, if you ask anyone out there who has accomplished anything in their life; they will tell you that they had help from someone else. They couldn't do it all themselves. Take a football team for example. A football team can only work if all 11 men on the field are working together, working in sync with one another, at the same time.

Let's start at the beginning. You have the "center," the person who first touches the ball. That center has to scope out the defense. When they line up, the center has to make sure all the other linemen know who to block, know where the blitz may be coming from, and know where the covers may be. They have to see that right then and there.

The guards on the left and the right need to make sure they are keying what they are supposed to key. If they see that a linebacker or a safety is coming from a certain point, they have to know who to block. If they know that they have to block down on a line, then they have to know what's happening. The tackles have to make sure to know if they have to hit a linebacker, to push the linebacker out, or to push the linebacker in, and make sure the play goes accordingly.

Then you have the backs. The backs have to make sure that they are keying their blocks, or that they are running through the right holes. If the hole isn't there, they have to make sure they know which way to bounce it; whether to bounce it in or to bounce it out. You have the tight end; the tight end has to know if he should get open for a pass, or if he needs to block down to protect the running back or the quarterback.

The wide receiver has the same obligation. They have to spread that field and create separation. They also have to make sure that they are in position to block for someone going down field. If the wide receiver doesn't do his job right, then the quarterback cannot do his.

The quarterback comes next, and his is the most important position. The quarterback has to know where each one of those guys is on every play. That quarterback has to know what each and every person's job is. The quarterback has to trust that each of those players is going to reach their goal and accomplish what they are supposed to do. If they do, then everything will work perfectly. The quarterback is who the center has to give the ball to, and that quarterback has to make sure the play is executed properly. The quarterback has to get the ball into the right person's hands. Before that, he also has to make sure that the offense is set and moving the way he wants it to move. He must make sure that everything is moving in sync. If one person out of those 11 does not do their job right, the whole play could blow up.

It only takes one person to ruin it. So, you see, you have to depend on people. If you are too prideful to depend on others, your whole life, business, goals, and dreams can blow up just like that football play (game). You have to swallow that pride and say, "I'm going to take it on the chin, and I'm going to ask someone to work with me. I'm going to get things done." If you don't, then nothing will get done. We cannot be everywhere, every time, for everyone. You are going to have to depend on other people.

Part of leadership is delegating and letting others take on the tasks that you may not be able to take on at that time. A leader develops other leaders. You may want to find someone who is another "you." If you don't you will never get things done, and you will always be stagnant because you're not growing. If you continue to do everything by yourself, you will remain stagnant, you are staying the same.

A prime example is basketball. They used to criticize Kobe Bryant all of the time saying, "Kobe wants to do everything himself. He doesn't trust his teammates. Until he trusts his teammates he won't win the big one without

Shaquille O'Neill." Once Shaquille O'Neill left, Kobe Bryant was the star of that team.

Kobe wanted to build a relationship with his teammates at that point, so he started taking everyone out for extracurricular activities outside of basketball in order to earn their trust. They began to like and trust him. They finally won two championships.

Those are the kinds of things that you have to do. Bryant swallowed his pride and realized, "It's not about me; it is about the team."

These things fall into play when you talk about business and life in general. You must get rid of the pride because it will eat you alive, and it will kill you if you let it. You cannot focus on, "You, you, you." It has to be an "us" thing.

You also have to understand that the people who come into your life to assist you are blessings. God puts them into your life for a reason, and when you say "no," you are blocking your blessings. You are taking away from whatever God has put in your path. You don't want to be in position where you cannot receive anything. If you cannot receive the blessing, then you cannot receive the benefit that comes from that blessing. You are basically right back to square one at that point.

Many years ago, Earnest Ainsley, a popular televangelist, wrote a book called "Untying God's Hands." To this very day I remember what that book was about. That book was very beneficial and important, and it talked about the fact that sometimes we have so much pride that we won't accept the blessings that are put in our way. If we try to take on every task God puts in our path by ourselves, then we miss the blessing.

If you say that you have been handling something for so long, and you don't accept help, then you have no idea what that help could bring to you. If you open your mind, open your heart, and open your eyes to see what that blessing has for you, you may be pleasantly surprised. You may get the things that you wanted, and more. So, don't block your blessings with your pride, because God has a plan and it is always awesome.

Guess what- they say if you want to make God laugh, tell Him your plans. Our plans are nothing compared to what God has planned for us.

Don't miss out on the bigger picture or you will miss out on what God has in store for you. God may be trying to get you to see another person's point of view on something. He could be doing it by bringing people into your life to help you. If you keep missing God, then you might be missing the fulfillment of your dreams.

Go ahead, and keep on being stubborn. Pride, like slothfulness, is another deadly sin. It will bring death to your dreams, your plans, your goals, and your main purpose in life. God cannot use someone who is prideful. It just isn't possible. You will continue to fall on your face because pride comes before a fall. If you continue to fall on your face, eventually you will be completely unusable, and you will never be able to get back to where you were. You might be able to start something new, but it won't be as great as the original path you were supposed to take.

Quotes About Pride

"Proud people breathe sad sorrows for themselves." (Emily Bronte – "Wuthering Heights")

"If you see anything in yourself which may make you proud, look a little further, you will find enough to make you humble. You have to have humility. Humility is going to be the key that is going to get you through life. If you are humble, you will start reaping benefits, because people respect humility. People want to be around a humble person. People like to know that someone doesn't take themselves way too seriously." (Wellins Calcott)

"There is a paradox in pride. It makes some men ridiculous, but prevents others from becoming so." (Charles Caleb Colton)

"Vanity and pride are different things. Though the words are often used synonymously, a person may be proud without being vain. Pride relates more to our opinion of ourselves, vanity to what we would have others think of us." (Jane Austin- "Pride and Prejudice")

"And the devil did grin, for his darling sin, his pride that apes humility." (Samuel Taylor Cooleridge- "The Devil's Thoughts")

"When a man's pride is thoroughly subdued, it is like the size of Mount Etna. It was terrible while the eruption lasted and the lava flowed. But when that is passed, the lava is turned into soil. It grows vineyards and olive trees up to every top." (Henry Ward Beecher)

"Pride juggles with her toppling towers. They strike the sun and cease. But the firm feet of humility, they grip the ground like trees." (G.K. Chesterton – "The Ballad of the White Horse")

"Pride is a cold, stormy, barren mountain." (John Thornton)

"The pride of the body is a barrier against gifts that purify the soul." (George Eliot)

"Pride is less ashamed of being ignorant, than of being instructed. She looks too high to find that what very often lies beneath us." (Charles Caleb Colton)

"Talent is God-given. Be humble. Fame is man-given. Be grateful. Conceit is self-given. Be careful." (John Wooden)

"Through pride we are ever deceiving ourselves. But deep down below the surface of the average conscience a still, small voice says to us, something is out of tune." (C.G. Jung)

"Humility is nothing but truth, and pride is nothing but lying." (St. Vincent de Paul)

"We are rarely proud when we are alone." (Voltaire)

"It often occurs that pride and selfishness are muddled with strength and independence. They are neither equal nor similar; in fact, they are polar opposites. A coward may be so cowardly that he masks his weakness with some false personification of power. He is afraid to love and be loved because love tends to strip bare all emotional barricades. Without love, strength and independence are prone to losing every bit of their worth; they become nothing more than a fearful, intimidated, empty tent lost somewhere in the desert of self." (Criss Jami)

"When you feel nervous, recall your pride." (Toba Beta)

"Wealth is a gift from God, and pride is bequeathed to us from the devil." (Douglas Wilson)

"Pride is a wound, and vanity is the scab on it. One's life picks at the scab to open the wound again and again. In men, it seldom heals and often grows septic." (Michael Ayrton)

"Maybe the truly handicapped people are the ones that don't need God as much." (Joni Eareckson Tada)

"In general, pride is at the bottom of all great mistakes." (John Ruskin)

"A competitor will find a way to win. Competitors take bad breaks and use them to drive themselves just that much harder. Quitters take bad breaks and use them as reasons to give up. It's all a matter of pride." (Nancy Lopez)

A Cautionary Tale –"C"

Cody was a person who was used to doing things, and having fun in life. He also had achieved a lot in his life. Cody would hobnob with stars and was invited to a lot of parties. All the ladies loved him, and he was very popular. His career was going great, he was making a lot of money, and he was traveling all over the world.

Then something happened. He got very ill; he got so ill that he spent most of his money paying for medicine and medical bills. Because he became so ill, all of his friends and the other people who had always wanted him around didn't want him around anymore. They knew Cody was sick. They knew that he couldn't do the things that he used to do with them, or for them.

Cody needed help from some of the same people whom he had helped before. But, he was too proud to call and ask them for help. Cody never went to those friends for anything again. They would still occasionally ask about him, and they would even call him, but he still wouldn't ask for help because his pride was too strong.

In the interim, his utilities were getting shut off; he stopped taking his medication, and his rent was not being paid. He got to a point where he had to make a choice to either pay rent or get his medicine. He decided to pay the rent, and not take the medicine because he couldn't afford it.

Cody died because he couldn't take care of himself, and his pride wouldn't allow him to ask for help. Don't be a proud person. Don't be a Cody.

Chapter 10 –
Feel the Fear

Fear is another huge obstacle that keeps people from accomplishing their goals. Fear gets in our way. Fear of the unknown or even fear of the known can paralyze us. We get afraid of things and cannot move. We cannot take a step forward, backwards, or even sideways. There is a saying that F.E.A.R. means "False Evidence Appearing Real." This basically means there is nothing to fear but fear itself.

If we tackle our fear, we realize it wasn't a big deal to begin with. The ideas that we put in our heads seem to grow and grow, and manifest themselves as something larger than life. Really, it wasn't that big of a deal to begin with. We laugh at ourselves afterwards, and say, "Why was I afraid of that?"

Think back to your childhood. There are a lot of things that you were afraid of, and as you grew older you were able to tackle them, and then you realized they weren't that big of a deal. A lot of times, fear is something that is taught. We are taught to be afraid of things. You can take a two year old child, and if he is by a swimming pool and sees a lot of people swimming, that child thinks he can jump in and swim right away. But once you start talking to the child about drowning and to be careful, because it is dangerous to jump into the water, then all of a sudden that child becomes fearful of the water, and they won't ever want to jump in.

We use fear in business to keep us from doing things. Fear is a big ugly monster that is always waiting around the corner to scare us. We think he is gone, but at the last second, "poof," there he is, and you jump out of your skin.

Fear is picking up the phone to call people. In business, this can be the biggest fear for some people. That phone weighs 800 pounds to them.

What is fear? Fear is the thing that keeps you from doing your best; it is the thing that keeps you from accomplishing things that you know you should be accomplishing. Fear is the one thing that can make or break your career or even your life. So, you have to be very careful as to how you approach fear. You can't let it consume you.

Fear is defined as a distressing emotion aroused by impending evil, pain, or danger. Whether the threat is real or imagined, it is the feeling or condition of being afraid. Fear is also considered to be a concern, or anxiety. Fear is something that we cannot let consume us, or we will become stagnant. We won't be able to accomplish anything.

What do we usually fear? We usually fear failure. No one likes to feel that they cannot accomplish something. No one likes to fear that they won't achieve.

Or, maybe you fear success. You probably say, "I don't fear success; I want to succeed." You'd be surprised at how many people fear success. With success comes obligations, responsibility and criticism. Success can be one of the most fearful things in life.

Those who fear success are often afraid of being separated from everyone else. We want to be like everyone else sometimes to feel like we aren't alone. When we become successful, we arrive at a different plateau, or a different level. We are separated from everyone else, and from that which is familiar.

When you reach that point, you have to maintain that level, otherwise you will fall back. If you fall back then you become afraid of being ridiculed for having failed. Either way, there will always be something in life to fear.

Everyone wants to achieve success. Maybe you just need to prove those doubters wrong in the end. No matter how long it takes for you to be successful, you have to get a handle on fear. How do you know what is coming if you haven't started your journey yet? You don't know what is waiting for you around that bend. You may have plans, and you may even be looking your goal right in the face. Things may change, and they may even turn out better than expected. But, for now, if fear is gripping your heart, push past it. Eventually it will have no other option but to let go.

Fear can drive us into either the success realm or the failure realm. We have to hone into what we want and go through the fear, be courageous, and get to our goals. Whether you become successful, or whether you fail at the beginning, you have to go through some type of fear to get where you want to be in life. Fear is just a feeling, and you don't have to give into your feelings. If you are living by your feelings, then you are surely weak, indeed.

You must live by faith, alone. Faith always births action (If it doesn't, it wasn't real faith to begin with). Are you ready to give birth? Are you ready to go through labor pains in order to receive the joy that awaits you around the corner? A pregnant woman has great joy, even in the midst of the pain, because she believes that she will have a bundle of joy in her hands very shortly and all of the pain will have been more than worth it. You can have joy, even while facing your fears and pushing those fears out of you with all of your will power.

You can do it. You can achieve. It always gets the roughest and the most painful right before the deliverance is complete.

Another part of fear is failure, or the fear of it. Don't be afraid to fail. If you are afraid of failure, then you have already failed. Always remember that failure comes with a lesson. You learn more from failing then you do from succeeding. You have to remember that you will eventually succeed, and when you do, you will feel the pleasure of that success. You will feel amazing. But, you have to work at seeing failure as a learning experience, something worthwhile. If you put forth an effort, and do your best, but don't succeed in meeting a particular goal, you shouldn't be afraid. Embrace it, learn from it, and move forward.

You want to continue to see failure as a learning experience, even if you fail 100 times. Albert Einstein failed more than 100 times, and what he eventually accomplished for all of mankind was amazing. There is a great self-help coach by the name of Tom Hopkins. He has written many books, and "How to Master the Art of Selling" is one that comes to mind. He talks about never seeing failure as merely failure but as a learning experience. One thing he says is, "I never see failure as failure, but as the feedback that I need to change course in my direction." He also says, "I never see failure as failure, but only as an opportunity to improve my sense of humor." You have to learn to laugh at yourself and stop taking everything so seriously.

Another truism spoken by Hopkins is, "I never see failure as failure, but only as an opportunity to practice my techniques and to perfect my performance.

Whatever you see or don't see is temporary, anyway. It will all fade away someday, and you will look back and see the insanity of your fears. Don't be insane! Fear causes insanity in more than one way. You see so many people with O.C.D. or different phobias who become only more afraid and insane as time goes on. They also never learn how to face their fears and they become stuck forever. They become recluses. Is that what you want, to become a recluse: To live knowing only your fear and nothing else, rejecting the pain that caused it, instead of accepting it and allowing yourself to change because of it? Are you going to continue to allow it to become a part of who you are?

I think not!

Get it through your head, "You are not your fear."

Lastly, Hopkins says, "I never see failure as failure, but only as the game I must play to win." If you keep in mind- all of the time- that failure always brings an opportunity, then you won't fear it. You will take it on. Yes, there may be some anxiety attached to it and maybe some "butterflies" in your belly. If you have butterflies- it's good- it keeps you focused.

I used to perform as a singer in a band. I always had a little anxiety before I went on stage. The butterflies kept me focused, yet I was clear in my mind, I remembered what I had to sing every time on stage. If I got too relaxed, I might forget the song. I have seen many artists forget the words. I've even seen artists who forgot the words to a song that they wrote because they weren't focused. Susan Jeffers authored a book titled, "You Have to Feel the Fear and Do It, Anyway." As long as you can do that- don't let the fear consume you, you will be in a very good position.

Now, there are a couple ways to overcome fear. But you have to make sure you do something to overcome it. You can't just sit around waiting for a miraculous deliverance of your troubling emotions. It just won't happen. In order to conquer fear, you have to be realistic. You may or may not overcome it all at once. You have to take small steps at first, and once you get better at it, then you can start taking bigger steps. You want to make sure that you identify the root of your fear–what your true fear is.

You may be afraid for reasons altogether different from what you originally thought you were afraid of. You have to dig deep, down to that root, to find out where the fear is coming from. Think of an old memory that may be related to it, accept what happened, grieve the hurtful event, and move out of the fear. Who knows, after you fully release that pain, the fear may dissipate altogether.

You also need to weigh out the pros and cons: What are the benefits and consequences if you don't tackle this and face your fear somehow, some way? If you don't face it, what will happen? What is the worst-case scenario? What are the consequences going to be if you don't face it? If you aren't sure, it is very possible that you will miss out on a lot in life. You may even miss out on your dreams completely.

The truth is, if you don't heal from the cause of your fear, it will follow you around forever. It will always be sitting there at the top of your emotional surface and become the cause of other emotional issues such as anger, depression, anxiety, and false pride. We have already delved into the subject of what pride can do to you. Most pride is actually buried deep down inside with fear as a "mask."

You have to take action. You must do something no matter how small. You may have to take a leap of faith.

If you just do something, you will find out that it wasn't so bad to begin with. Finally, as crazy as it seems, you want to put yourself in a no-way-out situation. You have to put yourself into a situation where you don't have any other choice but to attack your fear. You need a situation where there is no way that you can step back and say, "There's no way I can do it now." It's win or bust baby. You just have to go get it. Go get the fear; go after it with all you are. Leave yourself no options.

We fear not being perfect. We fear that if we are not perfect, we cannot be the winner or the achiever we want to be. No one is perfect, not even you. Even if you think you're perfect, you are not, and you never will be. So, don't put that kind of pressure on yourself.

We also fear our past; we've had trying and traumatizing events that have happened, and they keep us from getting things done. Have you been in a traumatizing relationship? An abusive relationship, whether it is physical or verbal keeps you from going into the next relationship, because you are afraid that the next person will be just like the others. Well, what ends up happening is that you spend your life unhappy because you won't step out and give something a shot.

Some of us are afraid of not achieving high enough. Maybe you have achieved something, but you want to achieve more–not necessarily at a level of perfection. You aren't always going to achieve everything, but at least you can say that you got out there and did it, and accomplished something. Some people don't even do that because of their fear.

Some of us fear criticism. We don't like having someone tell us that we aren't great. We don't like having someone tell us that we did something wrong. Sometimes criticism can be the best thing for us. It can make you better because you want to work harder. Here's an example from the life of Michael Jordan: When he tried-out for his high school basketball team, his coach said he wasn't good enough, and cut him. Well, you all know the rest of that story. Jordan wasn't afraid; he took it as a challenge to make himself better.

If you focus on the problem it will only bring you more problems; but if you focus on the solution, you will conquer your fear, and everything will be solved quickly.

"Anxiety never solved a problem; we do." (Author Unknown) If you continue to ruminate in your mind, you will get lost, and your mind surely isn't an easy place to find one's way out of. No one has a map. No one, except for God, can see into our minds. We cannot even see into our own minds entirely. This is a battle between you and your fear. No one else can fight it for you.

Quotes About Fear

"In order to succeed, your desire for success should be greater than your fear of failure." (Bill Cosby)

"Expose yourself to your deepest fear. After that, fear has no power. The fear of freedom shrinks and vanishes. You are free." (Jim Morrison)

"We gain strength, and courage, and confidence by each experience in which we really stop to look fear in the face. We must do that which we think we cannot." (Eleanor Roosevelt)

"I learned that courage was not the absence of fear, but the triumph over it. The brave man is not he who does not feel afraid, but he who conquers that fear." (Nelson Mandela)

"I fear not the man who practiced 10,000 kicks once, but I fear the man who has practiced one kick 10,000 times." (Bruce Lee)

"If people are good only because they fear punishment, and hope for reward, then we are a sorry lot indeed." (Albert Einstein)

"People fear death even more than pain. It is strange that they fear death. Life hurts a lot more than death. At the point of death the pain is over. Yes, I guess it is a friend." (Jim Morrison)

"Action and reaction, ebb and flow, trial and error, change; this is the rhythm of living. Out of our over-confidence, fear; out of our fear, clear vision, fresh hope; out of hope, progress." (Bruce Barton)

"The whole secret of existence is to have no fear. Never fear what will become of you. Depend on no one. Only the moment when you reject all help, are you free." (Buddha)

"Courage is resistance to fear; mastery of fear, not absence of fear." (Mark Twain)

"Success is never final, failure is never fatal. It's courage that counts." (John Wooden)

"It takes courage to grow up and become who you really are." (E.E. Cummings)

"The most courageous act is still to think for yourself. Aloud." (Coco Chanel)
"Above all, be the heroine of your life, not the victim." (Nora Ephron)

"A ship is safe in harbor, but that's not what ships are for." (William G.T. Shedd)

"Life shrinks or expands in proportion to one's courage." (Anais Nin)

"Freedom lies in being bold." (Robert Frost)

"Bran thought about it. 'Can a man still be brave if he's afraid?' 'That is the only time a man can be brave,' his father told him." (George R.R. Martin, "A Game of Thrones")

"Without fear there cannot be courage." (Christopher Paolini)

"No matter how long you train someone to be brave, you never know if they are or not until something real happens." (Veronica Roth, Insurgent)

A Cautionary Tale – "U"

Meet Ursula, who wanted to join a network marketing business. She decided to ask her friend Sandy to join with her. Sandy said sure because they liked to do things together. Part of the job entailed them calling people and setting up appointments. Ursula didn't want to do this; she hated the phone, because she had a fear of people telling her "no."

Sandy had the same fear, but she said, "You know what, I'm going to give it a shot. If they don't like it, who cares, what are they going to do to me?" So, Sandy decided to call people, and Ursula didn't.

Sandy built up a large team of people, and she started teaching them how to make phone calls, and how to get things going. Her income grew to an exponential amount. Soon, she became financially independent. She went on several trips, and even took Ursula with her a few times. Ursula still never got on that phone.

Sandy became one of the most recognizable people in the whole company, and she built a career and a life that she never dreamt she would be able to achieve. Ursula ended up getting a nine-to-five job, at a minimal salary, never really achieving her dreams but wishing she could be like Sandy.

She never achieved her goals because she gave into her fear. Don't be an Ursula.

Chapter 11 –
Goals

If you want to dream big you have to make small goals along the way. You can dream in your sleep, so I don't put too much credence in dreams. A lot of people have dreams: Big dreams, small dreams, weird dreams, and crazy dreams. There are many types of dreams out there, but in order to see your dream become reality, to meet your goal, you have to put it on paper, create a sequence, and make it a commitment. Make it so others can see what you are doing– that it's not just something that you talk about all the time.

Eventually, if you keep dreaming, reality will kick in. Once reality kicks in, you'll discover that reality has a strange way of pushing your dreams aside. Think about it. Think about when you were younger and you had all of these dreams about what you wanted to do with your life. How you wanted to conquer the world, what you were going to do, how much money you were going to make, the type of person you wanted to marry, the number of children you wanted, the type of career you were going to have… These dreams were in your mind since you were a young child.

You had an idea of an entire future life, and then reality set in. Reality has a way of being very cruel, and it will give you one little setback that makes your life go into a tailspin, so that you snowball and snowball into a downward spiral. The next thing you know, you have forgotten all about those dreams. Or, you see someone else living out your dreams and you wonder - what happened?

What happened, and why did my dreams dissipate? Why is that other person living out my dreams? Where did it go wrong, when did go it wrong and why did it go wrong? You may even have a specific point of reference as to where everything went wrong, but it isn't too clear. Because it isn't clear, we start blaming other people.

Maybe you start saying your ex-boyfriend ruined your life, or all of your exes ruined your life. Or maybe you blame your parents and that is why you have so much resentment toward them and the pain they have caused you.

Blame and excuses aren't going to make your dreams come alive and it won't help if you go back in time to start over again. You now have so many questions that are plaguing your mind it seems nearly impossible to reach your dreams.

Reality can ruin everything you have ever dreamt of. You are probably wondering, "What is the point of having dreams at all if reality is going to continue to pop its ugly head out of the box?"

It is good to dream when we are young. Those youthful dreams allow us to look back at our innocence, our hope, and our determination. Even though reality set in at some point along the way, being able to have the same kind of limitless, childlike expectations is what humbles us as adults. It also gives us more of a serious passion to have great dreams, again- even if they aren't the same ones.

Even if reality has set in, it isn't too late. It is never too late.

Dreams may come and dreams may go, but the dreams you once had are still valid. You just haven't gotten out of your life of procrastination. You're continuing to let every unimportant thing get in your way. The bottom line is that you didn't break those dreams into smaller parts. You didn't set small goals for yourself, so that you would know exactly how close you are to reaching your dream.

Have you made your dreams important enough to fight for them? Are you willing to get into the middle of the boxing ring and have a match with whatever it is that is holding you back? Did you just assume that they were going to appear out of nowhere? Your dreams won't just miraculously appear. I'm sorry, but life doesn't work like that. Just like I stated in a previous chapter- you aren't going to wake up and find a million dollars on your bedroom floor. You have to work towards making that million.

There are many successful people in this world who have lived very hard lives, and you know what they did? They allowed their pain, suffering, struggles, and trials to shape them and move them toward something greater. They didn't just sulk and never move forward. You can trap yourself through "unforgiveness" and self-pity regarding your past and the people in it. What you need to do is accept what happened, stop blaming, forgive, and move on. Start planning your new life.

"Unforgiveness" is suicide. You are killing yourself through your own anger and the pain you insist on holding onto. You have a noose of unforgiveness tied around your neck, and you are the one who put it there.

Don't hold onto regrets. Cut the noose off of your neck. Learn from your past instead, and tell yourself that you wouldn't be the person you are today if you hadn't had those experiences. Whether you believe it or not, it is true for all of us who have gone through pain and tribulations in this life. You just have to think about the things you have learned, and allow yourself to glory in that learning. Allow that wisdom and knowledge to sink in, once again. Doing this will give you a greater sense of self-esteem; you will start to believe in yourself.

If you have a hard time forgiving those who have hurt you, then remember this: Forgiving them will heal you.

There is a saying, "He who angers you, controls you." You have the choice as to whether or not you are going to be controlled. The person who hurt you doesn't care if you are mad at them. They may not even remember what they did to you. The fastest way to forgive, even if it is hard for you, is to pray for that person.

Pray as often as you can. Pray about the pain they caused and allow it to come to the surface. If you still see the person who hurt you every now and then, be prepared ahead of time and give them something nice, or do something nice for them. At the very least, give them a compliment, no matter how hard that may seem. In doing these things, you will start to feel better and less angry. You will finally be able to move forward into the amazing future that God has planned for you since before the beginning of time.

You have to fight and put things in place. You create your future. You have to make the goals happen and put them into action. If you don't put them into action, they are nothing more than a fantasy.

We've all have had fantasies. How often do your fantasies come true? If they do, then you probably set a goal and put something into action. Or, you made a plan and worked that plan out until you accomplished what you wanted. Think about that for a second. Your finished goal won't just miraculously appear out of nowhere; you have to turn it from a dream into a goal.

Now, you have to understand, if you want to create your own reality, you are going to have to have goals, no matter what. You have to have the wherewithal to say, "I'm going to make this happen." Share it with other people, as well. Some people are afraid to share their goals with others because they don't want to be ridiculed, laughed at, or put down.

If you have the courage and conviction that you are going to make this happen, then go forward and tell other people. Who cares what they think. It's not their goal. Be brash enough to say, "I'm going to do this." Let them laugh, who cares if they laugh. You get the last laugh when you succeed. Use that as your drive to make sure you go forth and reach your goals.

Let the naysayers come; they will go just as quickly. I promise you, if you are serious and work your plans, they will go away because they will be intimidated by your persistence. If they aren't afraid, if they want to be involved because they know that they can help you - that alone is enough reason to tell others about your plans. There may just be that one person you need to help you waiting right there around the corner, but you won't know it if you haven't talked about your plans.

You want to create your own reality. Run after it, and tell people what you are going to do, and let them insult you, if they will. As a matter of fact, record them, and write down what they say to you. That way, when you reach your goal you can go back to them and say, "I told you so." That will put them in their place.

Eventually these same naysayers will be running after you, because you will be a positive influence on them. They will even try to deny their earlier put-downs, because many people talk out of their ass.

Realize that your goals come between dreams and reality. I always say that goals are the 'meat' in your dream and reality sandwich. They fit right in the middle there. You must make sure you have strong goals and a plan on how you intend to reach your goals. If you don't have a plan, you're not going to get there. You've heard that saying, "If you fail to plan, then you plan to fail."

If you don't have a plan, then you may as well give up on your dreams right now and stop reading this book. Don't put anything else in this book into action if you don't set goals. Go home and stay home, and rot forever. Is that what you want?

Take some time right now and write if you have to, so that you don't forget. Start writing about what you want to do, it is that simple. Even if you can only come up with one sentence, do it. Once you see it on paper, you will most likely get more ideas and continue writing. You may not even be sure how to write it down in totality, but all you have to do is start with one word. That is what writers have to do sometimes. If a writer gets "writer's block," they step away from the paper and relax their minds. They come back to it, and start with just one word or one phrase or sentence. After that, they just flow. You may have to give it some time, but don't continue reading this until you have a few sentences written down. Nothing will help if you don't take the time to write your goals and dreams on paper. You have to make sure that you can put yourself in position by fighting for your goals.

Dr. Edwin Locke, an American psychologist and a pioneer in goal-setting theory had a distinct and well-respected philosophy. He wrote an article, called, "Toward a Theory of Task Motivation and Incentives." In this article, he talked about how people try to encourage others to reach their goals. We always tell people that they need to try harder, and go forward and do their best. But that isn't a goal. It may be an ambition, but it isn't a goal. You can say, "Do your best, and do better than your last time." I've worked with people myself, where I've told them to set goals, but I wasn't specific enough with them. When I did that, they would set a small goal. I knew that goal wasn't big enough for them. But they wouldn't be courageous enough to expand it for themselves. So they kept the goal small; they kept something that they knew they could reach easily.

Yet, if you don't challenge yourself, if you don't make things difficult you won't ever grow. I remember when I was a kid. I wanted to play basketball, so my friends and I went to the basketball court, and there were always taller kids there. But our goal was to somehow beat them. We mapped out a plan; we wrote it out. We had to be creative. I developed a hook shot to get the ball over the taller guys. If I had made shots my usual way, it wouldn't have worked.

Sometimes you just have to be creative and think outside the box. Do something you normally wouldn't do to get there. Of course, you have to do more than just a hook shot. You have to do something that is going to set you apart from the rest of the crowd. Trying hard isn't enough. You have to go after your best; you must go after something that is better than your best. Here are the five essential principles that Dr. Locke spoke of regarding setting goals.

Dr. Locke's Five Principles

1) Clarity – You have to be clear and concise about what you want to do. It can't be immeasurable, and it cannot be ambiguous. It has to be something that you know you can shoot for and you have to be specific about it. If you aren't specific about your goals, you will end up in trouble. You will have no pattern, and nowhere to go. You have to have the end in mind and in sight. If you don't, you will be lost out in the ocean. That is why there are lighthouses, to guide those who are lost at sea. Use clarity as your lighthouse to reach your goals. You need to be able to have direction to accomplish your goals.

2) Challenge– You have to challenge yourself. You have to make it so that if you don't hit your goal, there is a consequence. You also have to make it so when you do hit your goal, there is a reward. In challenging yourself you ensure that the higher the challenge, the higher the reward or consequence. You may have to be more disciplined with yourself. You have to make it so you are achieving something greater than you have achieved before, and if you don't, then you must pay a greater price than before.

3) Commitment– Commitment is very special to me. Because I find a lot of people are afraid to commit. Most people have the most difficulty, are the most afraid, of committing to their children. Why is that? Because your children actually expect you to honor your word. They expect you to be honest. What a novel concept! Your children are basically going by what you teach them. You teach them to be honest with you, not to lie, to always tell the truth. You teach them to go after whatever they say they want out of life. You teach them that they can accomplish anything and that nothing is impossible.

Then, when you tell them your goals and your plans, they expect you to do the same thing. It's only human nature. Most of us know that if we put our butt on the line and tell our children we are going to do something, they expect us to do it. But most of us don't have the gumption to get on and do it.

Let me give you an example. Let's say that you have a young child, and you really need to get some work done. If you tell your child, "Hey, Johnny, if you allow Daddy to work harder over the next three months, I won't be able to spend as much time with you, but I promise you if I can get some things accomplished, I will have enough money to take you to Disney World when school is out for the summer." Do you think that little Johnny is going to forget that? Heck no. He is going to remember that every single day. He is going to tell everyone he knows. He will tell all of his friends, "My daddy is going to take me to Disney World when he finishes working, after school is out."

When you get home from work, Johnny is going to say, "Daddy, how close are we to going to Disney World?" "We are still going to Disney World, aren't we?" The bottom line is, most you are afraid to put your butt on the line, because you know that you were lying to your kid when you made that promise.

That's right I said it. You were lying to your kid when you made that promise. You have no intention of honoring your commitment to your child, and that's why you are afraid to say something like that to them. You're afraid that your kid will hold you to your word.

How sad it is that you would lie to your child. Why don't you stand up as a man or woman and honor your word? Do what you said you would do: Work to take that child to Disney World. They deserve it. You're the one being lazy. Get up off of your butt and go to work. Make a commitment to that work and to that child. You both deserve to have a vacation. You deserve to be speaking the truth; you deserve to be told the truth, and your child deserves to hear the truth, as well. That is what commitment is all about.

Another thing about commitment, your goals must be something that you agree upon. You must be ready to make a commitment to yourself. When you talk to someone about your goals, make a commitment. Make it something that you agree upon with someone else. This way you will be more motivated to achieve it, and keep your word. If you can do that then you are on your way.

4) Feedback - Someone needs to hold you accountable. Someone needs to be able to tell you that you didn't attack that goal the way you said you would, or that you did a great job. You need someone to be your accountability partner to check in with you on your goals to see if you are on target or not. You need someone to ask you questions to make sure you stay on task and focused on what you need to do. You cannot keep anything a secret. As I said earlier, you want to share your dreams with people. Some will care enough- a spouse, for example- to be there for you and keep you accountable.

5) Task Complexity – Your goals must have tasks attached to them. This will help you to actually accomplish things. Some are going to be more challenging than others, but you have to make sure that some are truly challenging and give yourself sufficient time to meet the goals, of course.

You also need to set aside some time to learn about how to accomplish goals. Keep in mind that most people aren't familiar with setting goals, and even being held accountable for them, so give yourself a little leeway on how to attack your goals.

Now, I'm going to give you a few quotes on goal-setting to inspire you. Most of these quotes are from athletes. Athletes are premier people in goal-setting. Most people think that athletes are just born that way, but no, every single athlete that you see out there has goals. They work hard at their techniques and goals.

Quotes About Goals

"If you want to achieve a high goal, you are going to have to take some chances." (Alberto Salizar)

"Leaders aren't born, they are made. They are made just like anything else: Through hard work. That is the price you will have to pay to achieve that goal, or any goal." (Vince Lombardy)

"Champions do not become champions when they win the event, but in the hours, weeks, months, and years they spent preparing for it. The victorious performance itself is really the demonstration of their championship character. (T. Allen Armstrong)

"Act like you expect to get into the end zone." (Joe Paterno)

"I do not try to dance better than anyone else. I only try to dance better than myself." (Michael Birishnokoff)

"Setting a goal is not the main thing. It is deciding how you will go about achieving it, and staying with that plan." (Tom Landry)

"Winning isn't everything, but wanting it is." (Vince Lombardy)

"Goals are the fuel in the furnace of achievement." (Brian Tracy)

"If you don't know where you are going, you might not get there." (Yogi Berra)

"If you're bored with life....If you don't get up every morning with a burning desire to do things....you don't have enough goals." (Lou Holtz)

"Far away there in the sunshine are my highest aspirations. I may not reach them, but I can look up and see their beauty, believe in them, and try to follow where they lead." (Louisa May Alcott)

"Aim higher in case you fall short." (Suzanne Collins)

"Whenever you want to achieve something, keep your eyes open, concentrate and make sure you know exactly what it is you want. No one can hit their target with their eyes closed." (Paulo Coelho)

"If you want to live a happy life, tie it to a goal, not to people or things." *(Albert Einstein)*

"We must walk consciously only part way toward our goal and then leap in the dark to our success." (Henry David Thoreau)

"What keeps me going is goals." (Muhammad Ali)

"While intent is the seed of manifestation, action is the water that nourishes the seed. Your actions must reflect your goals in order to achieve true success." (Steve Maraboli)

"Leaders live by choice, not by accident." (Mark Gorman)

"Not all dreamers are winners, but all winners are dreamer. Your dream is the key to your future. The Bible says that, 'Without a vision (dream), a people perish.' You need a dream, if you're going to succeed in anything you do." (Mark Gorman)

A Cautionary Tale – "S"

This tale is about Sheila. Sheila and her best friend Beth went to college together. They were both marketing majors and they both thought that they would do great things in life. They used to dream and daydream about what they were going to do with their big companies someday.

When they got out of college, Beth had everything written down, and planned out to a T. She even had a job when she left college. They were waiting for her. She had her entire 10 year plan written out, and it was as follows:

- What type of job she wanted
- When she was going to buy her first house
- When she was going to get married
- How many children she was going to have
- When she was going to have her first child
- What type of neighborhood she was going to live in
- Where she was going to live
- Where she was going to travel
- When she was going to start her own company

She had everything written down and worked toward each and every one. Beth had everything mapped out and accomplished all of these goals and then some.

Sheila never wrote anything down. Sheila became known as a dreamer. She always told people what she wanted to do, but she never did it. No one took her seriously. Sheila would always say that Beth was her best friend, that she was an executive in a marketing firm that she owned. Sheila said that Beth was "lucky" and that everything was handed to her.

She would give one excuse after another as to why Beth succeeded, but never looked inside to say:

- I never set goals
- I didn't work for my goals
- I didn't reach my goals

The moral of the story is to set your goals, work toward your goals, and reach your goals. Don't be a Sheila.

Chapter 12 –
Commit to the Cause

D o you know what it is to commit to something, or to dedicate your life to something? Is there something that you have wanted to do for a very long time, but just haven't started it yet? Or, have you started, but haven't finished yet and you keep making excuses? Every goal that you set, every dream that you have, and everything you want to achieve in life, if you aren't committed, you aren't going to get them done. Sometimes, you will get lucky and someone will step up and do something that will benefit you. But most of the time it is your commitment to cause that will make it work.

Let's take marriage for instance; you have to commit in order to make your marriage work. Even before you decided to get married, you had to commit to that relationship. You had to commit to your career choice in order to make it successful. You had to commit to your schoolwork in order to graduate. You might have eased through it, but there was a commitment along the way, otherwise you wouldn't have gone to class, you wouldn't have sat through lecture, and you wouldn't have studied.

You are either going to commit to failure or commit to success. You can commit to either one, but not to both. There are plenty of people who automatically commit themselves to failure because they lack a plan and they lack action. They don't put in the work; they don't learn what is necessary, and they don't put in the time. That is committing to failure.

In order to commit to success, you put in the work, you put in the time, and you put in the effort. You might as well make a conscious commitment to something because even if you don't, by default, you are going to commit.

You may say to yourself, "No, I'm not committing to either one." If that's the case, then you just committed to failure. It is your choice as to what you will commit to. If you don't proudly and with great honor say you are committed to success, then you have failed already. One way or the other you win or lose. Do you want to be a loser your whole life? It is your choice.

Now, let's look at commitment in more detail. You've all heard the expression about the eggs and the bacon, right? There is a chicken and there is a pig. One of them made a contribution to breakfast, and one of them made a commitment to breakfast. The chicken made a contribution. The pig made a commitment. He sacrificed his life. Which leads me to my point: Commitment requires sacrifice. You are going to have to sacrifice something. Ask yourself why you even want success, and remember; sacrifice and success go hand in hand. If you cannot sacrifice, then you don't deserve success. If you don't sacrifice, then you aren't going to see your goals in such a way that you will stay determined to get there.

It could be your time, your friends, your family, your career, a hobby, or someone with whom you spend most of your time that you must sacrifice. You must sacrifice something in order to commit. You also have to ask yourself if you have a "cause" or not. What is the cause that you are committing to? What drives you? Is there a crusade of some kind? Is there something making you say you have to do this? Is there something that you must do because, "someone needs you," or a family member that passed away "needs you to do this" in their name?

Maybe you are saying something like, "I have to do this because if I don't, there is a huge consequence on the other side." Whatever the cause, if you don't have one, you are flying without wings. You don't know where you are going; you won't have guidance, and nothing else will put you in the right place where you need to be. If you don't sacrifice, then you don't have a cause.

Jesus Christ was committed to a cause. Now, I'm not saying that you need to give up your life the way Christ did, but you do have to give up some aspect of your current "lifestyle." So, in a way, you are sacrificing your life. Christ had a cause- to let everyone know what His Father's Word said. What is your cause? What is going to make people notice you? What's going to make things happen for you? In what ways do you need to sacrifice your life?

As I said before, just as success and comfort don't mix, success and convenience don't mix, either. Things aren't going to be easy or happy-go-lucky. It isn't going to be roses and rainbows if you commit to something and really make it happen. A lot of people see entertainers, athletes, and politicians and say, "Wow, well they have it made." Whoever became successful in this world chose to commit to something and put in the required work. When you didn't see it happening, that is when it was happening. But, it wasn't easy, convenient, or comfortable for them. Success and comfort don't mix- remember that.

Success is a choice. You have to choose to give up your life. You have to choose to make that sacrifice for yourself. I want to make sure you understand that commitment is also something that will take you the next level. If you don't put in the time, you won't get to the next level. Do you get up in the morning thinking, "I must get this done today."? Do you get up in the morning thinking, "If I don't get it done, somebody is going to suffer, and it may be me."? Do you go to bed at night thinking, "I accomplished my goals today because I was committed to accomplishing those goals."? Or do you go to bed just wanting to go to sleep? There is a difference between being a winner and being a loser. As I said before, you either commit to winning or you commit to losing. The loser doesn't think about what sacrifices they have to make. The winner does. Every winner has a commitment. Every loser doesn't. Use it or lose it. Use your talents, gifts, learning, abilities, or lose them completely, forever.

Quotes on Commitment

"Unless commitment is made, there are only promises and hopes, but no plans." (Peter Drucker)

"Obstacles are those frightful things that you see when you take your eyes off of your goal." (Henry Ford)

"Commitment by its nature, frees us from ourselves. And while it stands us in opposition to some, it joins us with others similarly committed. Commitment moves us from the mirror trap of the self-absorbed with the self to the freedom of a community of shared values." (Michael Lewis)

"Once a man has made a commitment to a way of life he puts the greatest strength in the world behind him. It is something called we call heart power. Once a man has made this commitment, nothing will stop him short of success." (Vince Lombardi)

"The relationship between commitment and doubt is by no means an antagonistic one. Commitment is healthiest when it is not without doubt, but in spite of doubt." (Rollo May)

"Stay committed to your decisions, but stay flexible in your approach." (Tom Robbins)

"Commitment means that it is possible for a man to yield to the never center of his consent to a purpose or cause, a movement or an ideal, which may be more important to him than whether he lives or dies." (Howard Thurman)

"There's a difference between interest and commitment. When you're interested in doing something, you do it only when circumstances permit. When you're committed, you accept no excuses, just results." (Art Turock)

"I believe that any man's life will be filled with constant unexpected encouragement, if he makes up his mind to do his level best each day, and as nearly as possible reaching the high water mark of pure and useful living." (Booker T. Washington)

"Commitment unlocks the doors of imagination, allows vision, and gives us the "right stuff" to turn our dreams into reality." (James Womack)

"By 'hero', we tend to mean a heightened man, who, more than other men, possesses qualities of courage, loyalty, resourcefulness, charisma, and above all, selflessness. He is an example of right behavior, the sort of man who risks his life to protect his society's values, sacrificing his personal needs for those of the community." (Paul Zweig)

"If you don't make a total commitment to what you are doing then you start looking to bail out the first time the boat starts leaking. It's tough enough getting a boat to shore with everybody rowing, let alone when a guy stands up and starts putting his jacket on." (Lou Holtz)

"Until one is committed, there is hesitancy, the chance to draw back. Concerning all acts of initiative (and creation), there is one elementary

truth, the ignorance of which kills countless ideas and splendid plans: that the moment one definitely commits oneself, then Providence moves, too. All sorts of things occur to help one that would never otherwise have occurred. A whole stream of events issues from the decision, raising in one's favor all manner of unforeseen incidents and meetings and material assistance, which no man could have dreamed would have come his way. Whatever you can do, or dream you can do, begin it. Boldness has genius, power, and magic in it. Begin it now." (William H. Murray)

"A man can be as great as he wants to be. If you believe in yourself and have the courage, the determination, the dedication, the competitive drive, and if you are willing to sacrifice the little things in life and pay the price for the things that are worthwhile, it can be done." (Vince Lombardi)

"Football is like life – it requires perseverance, self-denial, hard work, sacrifice, dedication and respect for authority." (Vince Lombardi)

"When work, commitment, and pleasure all become one, and you reach that deep well where passion lives, nothing is impossible." (Author Unknown)

"You may have to fight a battle more than once to win it." (Margaret Thatcher)

"Desire is the key to motivation, but it's determination and commitment to an unrelenting pursuit of your goal – a commitment to excellence – that will enable you to attain the success you seek." (Mario Andretti)

"To finish first, you must first finish." (Rick Mears)

"We cannot be sure of having something to live for unless we are willing to die for it." (Ernesto "Che" Guevara)

"There's no scarcity of opportunity to make a living at what you love. There is only a scarcity of resolve to make it happen." (Wayne W. Dyer)

"There are only two options regarding commitment. You are either in, or you are out. There is no such thing as life in between." (Anonymous)

That last quote definitely sums up the point I want to get across: You must commit to something. Either winning or losing, good or evil, life or death, you are going to have to commit to something. You cannot commit by word, only by your actions. If you don't do it, you will surely pay for it. How much will you pay? So much that you cannot even put a price on it.

Your life is priceless. Sacrificing your life for doing something worthwhile is priceless. You won't always be here. You could be gone tomorrow. Don't wait. If you are, the only investment you will ever have made is going to be waiting for you at the graveyard. It will be too late once you have passed through to the other side. While you are still on this side, do something. Invest in your life. Invest your time, your money, everything you have. Your return will far outweigh what you put into it.

A Cautionary Tale – "E"

Edna was a single mother and she had a son who was becoming a young man. She was very proud of him, and therefore wanted to be a good example for him. She had a business of her own. She worked her business so well showing her son that one day he could do the same and be even better at it than she was. But, Edna ended up getting into a rut; she stopped doing the activities that brought in business. She didn't stay committed. She noticed her check was getting smaller and smaller. She noticed that she was spending more time with her son, because she didn't have much business. She got comfortable and loved spending time with her son and figured that was good anyway.

Eventually, since she didn't have much income, she started borrowing money. She wouldn't seek clients or work at the business, because she couldn't afford to put gas in her car. She was getting too lazy about getting things done and kept doing these little things that were hurting her life. Finally, Edna was evicted from her apartment, because she couldn't pay her rent. She couldn't take care of her son, anymore, either. Edna's mother started taking care of her son- just until she got back on her feet.

Edna never got out of that cycle. She wasn't able get a place to live again and became homeless. Living on the street, she never got her son back, and her son never knew what it was like to achieve anything in life. The cycle continued. Please, don't be an Edna.

Chapter 13 –
It's all in the
Follow Through

The last question is how are you going to follow through? What do you think you need to do to get started? Maybe you need to read this book once more, but this time, get a notebook and a pen and go through each chapter slowly. Get everything you can out of this book. As you take notes, do whatever you think you need to do. Ask yourself some questions, and answer them. Do the hard work.

If you don't follow through, all of the other chapters you just read mean nothing, zero, zilch, nada. Now is the time to pull it all together and decide if you need to find a coach. Finding a coach is like finding a counselor. Not every coach out there is going to be the perfect match for you. You also have to be ready to be coached. If you are willing to re-read this book, that shows you are ready to follow through with your plans to reach your goals, to see your dreams to fruition, and I would consider coaching you.

As I've told you, I am a coach, but I don't coach just anybody. I only coach those people who are ready to follow through. There are some coaches who are going to coddle you and some who will work out a plan for you. Other coaches will merely listen to you. Then there are coaches like me: I am an action coach. I'm going to make you do it, and if you don't do it, I'm going to slap the hell out of you, and ask you why you didn't do it.

You're going to have to be accountable to something, and you are going to have to follow through at some point in your life. It doesn't matter if its business or your family; whatever you are dealing with, you are going to have to follow through. Think about it. How many times have you looked at your body and said, "I'm going to have to start working out to get myself back into shape." Did you notice that when you woke up the next morning those pounds didn't just go away? You have to actually follow through and make it happen.

I bet many of you have a girlfriend and you say to yourself, "You know what, I really would love to marry this woman, and I have to propose to her at some point." Did you notice the next time you saw her that the ring wasn't on her finger? At some point you are going to have to follow through. You are going to have to make that happen.

How about the time when you said, "I'm going to have to work harder so I can get that promotion the next time they give out promotions. Did you notice the next day that you went into work you didn't have a corner office? You have to follow through and work to make it happen. If you don't, it's not going to happen. Plain and simple, it's not going to happen.

You must follow every step that is laid out, and then put those steps into action. You have to get moving and stay moving. Don't stop until you reach the top. If you don't you will live your life filled with regrets. The graveyard is the wealthiest place in the world, because there are millions of people who died with plenty of ideas and dreams, but never followed through. There are so many great ideas that are probably going through your head even now. I know that you have talked about them time and time again, and you have figured out ways that you can capitalize on great opportunities.

Maybe you have thought about ways that you can make things happen, and ways you can make yourself into a stellar person in your family, community, and in the world. But if you don't follow through, it means nothing. You have to take advantage of what's been presented to you. Life has so many great opportunities, but nothing is going to happen unless you take a step toward it.

You've heard this before, so this is nothing new: You have got to do what you have got to do. Sometimes it takes a little sacrifice, sometimes it takes more than you expected. You might have to become an insomniac for a little while in order to have the time alone that you need to contemplate. Maybe you need to incorporate some meditation into your life so that your mind will become clear enough to hear what the universe is telling you.

Meditation is a well full of answers, solutions and peace. When you quiet your mind by force, you can access that well. The only way to bring up a full bucket is to stay quiet, contemplative for a certain period of time, say 20 minutes, and keep your mind at peace. Do this, and no matter how hard it is at first, eventually you will get better at it. Your wheels don't have to constantly spin in circles to find answers. Spinning your wheels actually makes it more difficult to find the answers you need.

However, you can find the answers through the spirit realm, through meditation, because it is there where everyone's spirits are connected. We are all one, whether you know it or not, whether you believe it or not, and whether you can see it or not.

To find answers in the spirit realm, you must access God through meditation. Psalm 46:10 says, "Be still and know that I am God." He has abundant wisdom, knowledge, and solutions. As quoted before, anxiety doesn't solve problems. It never has and it never will. It actually makes life more difficult because your mind becomes cluttered like a pack-rat's home.

We are all interconnected through One Spirit, so whatever someone needs from you, whatever you can give back to the world, can be found through silence.

We all need what you have. You need what we have. That is exactly why you got this book and read it. You needed the knowledge, inspiration, and wisdom that I was able to bestow upon you. You may continue to need more in the future. If so, that is why I am here and available to coach you, but only if you are ready to follow through.

If you don't follow through you will undoubtedly make life very difficult for yourself. I work in an arena, where in order to be a new business; you have to get a state license. I trained a young man, who came into the business and worked very hard. I have to give him a lot of credit for that, but he just couldn't pass the state test to get his license. He tested again and again, and finally, after he took the test seven times, he passed it. I know that a lot of people would have quit, but he didn't; he had the persistence and exceptional fortitude to go forward and get that license. This person had what we call "follow through." That's what we are looking for.

I know many of you reading this are probably saying that it was great that he kept taking the test even though he had failed so many times. You are probably thinking this guy does have what it takes, so what happened? Well, guess what? Once he got the license, he had no follow through. He didn't use the license, after all. All of that struggling, testing and failure to rise up in order to make it into something that was positive meant nothing, because he never followed through. He didn't make any money or do any business with that license. So it was totally a waste of time. Seven times he tested only to result in nothing, culminate in nothing. There was nothing gained from his efforts.

You must understand that if you don't act on what you learn, then you are just a vessel of information. We pick up a lot of knowledge and information in our lives. Some of you go to school for years, and years, and years. You study under great professors, and you have three or four degrees. You like to tell people that you have this degree and that degree and that you have a bachelor's degree, a master's degree in business, and a P.H.D. I'm sure many of you have heard that statement that everyone has a P.H.D: a Public High school Diploma. Don't worry about whether or not someone has a degree or a license. If they have a degree but aren't using it, it means nothing. If you call yourself a Doctor of Cardiology, but are now on a golf tour, then you're a golfer. Who cares if you are a doctor? You aren't opening up hearts right now. No one cares if you say that you are a doctor. If you are there to golf, then that is what they care about– golfing.

So many people keep obtaining information and keep reading and listening to the information and studying, but they never use that information. There is a difference between knowledge and wisdom. Anyone can get knowledge, and we all have some knowledge. Wisdom is applied knowledge. You have taken your knowledge and are using it. If you are truly wise, then you have followed through with something.

It is the same thing when you turn your dreams into goals. That is one step in following through. Now, you have to turn that goal into an accomplishment. If you don't accomplish anything, that goal just sits there and becomes stagnant. I will put it in real life terms for you:

Let's look at it like soccer. You have the goal at the end of the field, you have a soccer ball, and you have soccer players. If you are standing in front of the goal, and the ball is right there at your feet yet you don't kick the ball into the goal, then your team doesn't score. So, you have to follow through and score for your team otherwise you lose, and you lose big.

One of the best examples I have seen of people not following through is those who are real estate investors. I know this story, because I've seen it personally. If you have gone to a real estate investment seminar, then you will understand exactly what I'm referring to. Follow through is really exemplified when people get one of those Carlton Sheets, at-home study courses, that says you can buy a house with no money out of your pocket and no credit of your own. It is true, absolutely true. Most people will get this at home-study course, for $200. They finally have it in their possession, but it just sits there right on their desk or their shelf. They may even look at it, take out a couple of books or DVDs, review it once or twice but never follow through.

On the other hand, you may know someone who, all of a sudden, became rich through real estate investing. And you wonder what they did, what are they doing differently? It's not a different course, or a different teacher, or different information. It is only because they followed through. I've seen the same thing in other real estate investment situations and have actually seen the DVD sitting on someone's shelf.

It's the same thing with the weight loss programs and exercise videos. You buy an exercise video. It is sitting at home, and you use it for about a week. The next thing you say, "I don't want to do it today, and I don't want to do it tomorrow either." That is a prime example of NOT following through.

Here is an example of my own lack of follow through: I was in a car accident a while ago and I injured my back. My lawyer told me to go to a Chiropractor, so I went. The chiropractor was very good. He went over my x-rays and my MRI. and told me what I needed to do for therapy. I started to do everything he recommended, and then I stopped. The thing with any kind of injury, and I think all of you know this, is that you have to give it time to heal. Well I didn't give it time to heal, because I didn't follow through with therapy. So what happened, periodically, my back would start hurting me. I didn't get healed properly.

Finally, I said, "I'm going to follow through this time because I'm in serious pain." "I'm going to go to a chiropractor," and when I followed through, I began to see the results that I wanted. It's as simple as that; you have to follow through in order to make things happen. If you don't, you won't see results.

Everyone will have obstacles come their way that keep them from following through. You can call these obstacles different things: Friends, family, jobs, bills, hobbies, emergencies, or eating good food. If Jesus, Himself, said that we must leave homes or brothers or sisters or father or mother or wife or children or lands, for His name's sake in order to receive a hundred-fold (Matthew 19:29), then we surely must overcome obstacles in our lives to follow through and receive a return on our investment. That is what Jesus meant by "receiving a hundredfold." You may have to "leave" your family in order to provide for them, and I'm not only speaking of a nine-to-five job here, either. You may have to move to a different location in order to access what or who you need in your life.

You have to have that intentional fortitude and say, "I'm going to fight through it. I'm going to do this no matter what anyone says, even my family." If your family truly loves you, they will let you go. Allowing someone that freedom is what real love is. If you don't fight through to the other side, then you won't win. The obstacles will get in your way challenging you, pushing you to another level. If you don't fight, you don't win. Always keep that in mind. If you do, then you will be fine. **NO MORE EXCUSES!**

"If you always make excuses to not follow through, you deserve the weight of anxiety on your chest." (Daniel @blindedpoet)

A Cautionary Tale – "S"

Scott was the quarterback on a football team. He was very much a team player. He fully believed that in order to win the game, one must be a team player, and everyone must follow through. There were two football teams playing each other. One team was known for running the ball, and the other team was known for throwing the ball. The team that was known for throwing the ball was losing.

Thankfully, Scott was on the "running" team, even though they were winning, they were only up by four points at the half. The "throwing" team switched things up and started running instead of passing. They still had trouble in the second half, yet, took a slight lead after a touchdown on a kickoff return. But they couldn't get their new game plan going.

Scotts' team that ran the ball stayed with their philosophy, and they committed the second half of the game to running. They kept running, kept running and eventually they wore down the other team. They ended up scoring two touchdowns at the end of the game and won.

The point I'm trying to get across is, if you follow through with everything you planned from the very beginning and work it until the wheels fall off, then you will always be a winner in the end.

Barrett Matthews and Les Brown

Barrett Matthews and
Tom "Big Al" Schreiter

Barrett Matthews
and Willie Jolley
holding Dwattle
bottle created
by Barrett.

More Books From

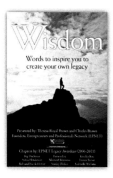

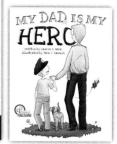

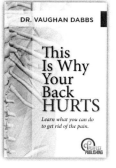

Your

Book

Here

www.PerfectPublishing.me